HEGEL
ENCYCLOPEDIA OF PHILOSOPHY

HEGEL
ENCYCLOPEDIA OF PHILOSOPHY

Translated and annotated by
GUSTAV EMIL MUELLER

PHILOSOPHICAL LIBRARY
New York

Printed in the United States of America

ACKNOWLEDGMENT

I want to thank my friend and colleague, Dr. J. Clayton Feaver, Kingfisher College Professor of Philosophy of Religion and Ethics at the University of Oklahoma, for his generous and careful reading of the manuscript and for many helpful critical suggestions.

CONTENTS

Translator's Note   1
Georg Wilhelm Friedrich Hegel   8

FOUR INTRODUCTIONS

Liberal Education: Preparation for Philosophy   43
Preface (1817)   54
From the Inaugural Address (1818)   57
From the Preface of the Second Edition (1827)   62

THE ENCYCLOPEDIA OF PHILOSOPHICAL SCIENCES

Dialectic and factual sciences §1-§11   67

THE LOGIC OF PHILOSOPHY

Systematic Introduction §12-§17   81
Historical Introduction §18-§36   85
The Beginning §38   97

QUALITY

Being §39   103
Negativity or Freedom §40   103
Origin §41   104
Omnipresence §42   105

Reality §43   105
Self-alienation §44   106
Endlessness §47   106
Infinity §48   107

QUANTITY

The Absolute as quantity §52   111
Continuity and discreteness §53   111
The quantum §54   112
Number §55   112
Extensive and intensive magnitude §56   112
Identity not equality §57   112
Quantity and quality §58   113
Measure and Measurelessness §59-§62   113
Essence of Reality §63   113

ESSENCE

"Is" and "seems" §64   117
Mediation of being and seeming §65   117
Concrete identity §66   117
Identity and difference §67   118
Dialectical relationalism §68   118
Internal and external relation §69   119
Being in-itself and for-itself §70   119
Dialectical position and opposition §71   119
Dialectical affirmation and negation §72   120
A is Non-A §73   120
Essence and existence §74   120
Determination and indeterminacy §75   121
Being and having §76   121
Problematic reason §77   121
Essential and unessential §78-§80   121
Essence appears §81   122
Existentialism §82   122
Dependent, independent, interdependent §83   122
The Struggle §84   122

Being is essentially Life §85   123
The psycho-physical dialectic §86   123
Inner and outer §87   124
Self-manifestation §88   124
Psycho-physical dualisms §89   124
Actuality (Wirklichkeit) §90   124
Dialectical unity of opposites §91   124
Actuality and possibility §92   125
Contingency §93   125
Decision §94   125
Potential and actual §95   125
Necessary Being §96   126
Substance and accident §97-§98   126
Value §99   126
Sufficient Cause §100   126
Creativity §101   126
The Concept (Begriff), Substance is Subject
  §102-§106   127
Self-knowledge §107   128
Truth §108   128

THE CONCEPT

Identity of Subject/Object §109   133
Freedom and necessity §110   133
Subjective appropriation of objective content
  §111   133
Cause of itself §112   134
Concrete identity and concrete universality §113   134
Self-criticism §114   135
Life as task §115   136
Self-differentiation of universal, particular and
  individual §116   136
The Concept in its immediacy §117   137
The Logic of the "Judgment" (Ur-Teil)
  §118-§128   137
Comprehension (Vernunft) §129   138
The "speculative conclusion" (Vernunftschluss)
  not a formal-logical syllogism §130   138

Forms of the speculative "syllogism" §131-§134   139
Mathematical measuring not logical §135   140
Induction and analogy §136   140
Reason (Verstand) as "moment" of Comprehension (Vernunft) §137-§138   140
The ontological argument: Proof of the subject/objectivity of the "Concept" §139   141

The Idea

Final Cause §140   147
Objectivism or realism §141   147
Formal mechanism §142   147
Irrationalism of both §143   148
Negativity in nature §144   148
Absolute mechanism §145   148
Attraction and repulsion §146   148
Chemism §147   148
Tendency towards harmony §148   149
Reciprocity of action/reaction §149   149
External Image of Life §150   149
Drawn into Life §151-§152   149
Intentionality and teleology §153   149
External and internal purpose §154-§155   150
Subjective end and objective means §156   151
Mechanism and chemism subordinated to purposive activity §157   151
The "Cunning of Comprehension" §158   152
Intelligible objectivity/objective intelligibility §159-§160   152
The Absolute as free, eternal self-determining actuality ("The Idea") §161   152
Totality of all dialectical correlations §162   153
The individual participates §163   154
Interpenetration of universal, particular, and individual §164   154
Concerns and realms of Life:
Immortality §165   155

Dissolution §166   155
Procreation §167   155
Natural and spiritual life §168   156
Freedom from and freedom for §169   156
Negative and positive freedom §170   156
Ontology terminates in self-knowledge; self-
    knowledge is ontologically significant §171   156
Comprehension beyond reason §172   157
Dialectics and analytics §173   157
Analysis and synthesis §174   157
Philosophy: living mirror of Idea §175   158
Divisions of Philosophy necessary §176   158
Pseudo-dialectic ("arbitrary constructions") and
    formal "isms" §177   158
The absolute process in will §178   158
Truth and goodness §179   159
Self-contradiction of the will §180   159
"Ought" versus "is" §181   159
The absolute good never is experience;
    reconcilation of finite contradictions with
    the Absolute §182   160
The Absolute available §183   160
It is both origin and end §185   160
The process of mediation §186   161
Present on all levels §187   161
Denies abstract beginnings or final results §188   161
Comprehensive process in many teleological
    wholes §189   161
There is one Universe §190   162

Philosophy of Nature

Introduction: Nature as Idea in the form of
    self-estrangement §192-§196   165
Mathematics, Space-Time, Matter as energy
    §197-§212   167
Physics §213-§250   174
Chemistry §251-§259   179

The Earth §260-§265 181
The Plant §266-§272 182
The Animal §273-§298 185

PHILOSOPHY OF THE SPIRIT

Introduction (from second edition) §377-§386 191
The natural Soul §307-§327 197
Subjective Mind §329-§344 207
Self-consciousness §345-§368 213
Subjective Mind as theoretical §369-§387 221
Subjective Mind as practical §388-§398 227
Objective Mind, Introduction §482-§487
 (2nd edition) 234
Legality §402-§415 236
Morality §416-§424 240
Social Ethics (Sittlichkeit) §430-§441 244
Philosophy of History §442-§449 254
Transition from objective mind to absolute
 spirit §552 (4th edition) 259

ABSOLUTE SPIRIT

Introduction §453-§454 269
Art §456-§464 270
Religion. Introduction from Propädeutik
 §71-80, §207; §465-471 276
Philosophy §472-§477 284

HEGEL
ENCYCLOPEDIA OF PHILOSOPHY

TRANSLATOR'S NOTE

To translate the world's worst stylist literally, sentence by sentence, is possible—it has been done—but it is perfectly pointless; the translation, then, is every bit as unintelligible as the original. But the world's worst stylist is, alas, also one of the world's greatest thinkers, certainly the most important for us in this twentieth century. In the whole history of philosophy there is no other single work which could hold a candle to his *Logic;* a work incomparable in its range, depth, clarity of thought, and beauty of composition—but it must be decoded.

The attempt must be risked, therefore, to rescue its grandeur from its abstruse linguistic chaos. I have dared to translate—not the ponderous Hegelian jargon, which is as little German as it would be English —but the thought. My "translation," then, is a critical presentation or rendition; it is not a book about Hegel because it faithfully follows the order and sequence of his own paragraphs.

This is like detective work: What Hegel means, but hides under a dead heap of abstractions, must be guessed at and ferreted out. Clues are often found in some words, in some elucidating remarks, or in footnotes added from his lectures. To explain or defend in each case what I have found to be the core of the paragraphs would require several volumes of philological discussion. The only proof which I could offer for the correctness of my guesses is the inner coherence of each paragraph with the preceding and succeeding ones. Hegel has always claimed that there is a necessary sequence and development in his *Logic;* I have finally convinced myself that this claim is true.

There are, as I see it, five difficulties in Hegel's language:

1. The first difficulty is quite objective and lies in the nature of his philosophy. There simply are no words in the language—whether English or German —which are capable of expressing his concrete thinking. Since he nevertheless must have some terms, he takes them from the ordinary language but uses them in a new and original way.

Take, for example, the second section of his *Logic,* entitled *Wesen.* The dictionary gives the following English equivalents: "Being, existence, reality; essence; being, creature, living thing; state, condition; nature, character, disposition; intrinsic virtue; conduct; organization; system, arrangement, concern." Hegel uses all of these meanings, but at the same time clasps them in an over-all new meaning: *Wesen* is the essence of Being, and Being was discovered in the first section of his *Logic* to be a dialectical structure. It is a unity of immediacy and mediation, of origin and omnipresence, of quality and quantity, etc. When Being is known as this unity of its opposites, it is known in its essence. Essence, thus, is the dialectical nature of Being together with the development of this nature.

The next section of the *Logic* is called *Begriff.* The dictionary meaning of "Begriff" is the ordinary logical "concept" which is a class or a kind of its many instances. But for Hegel the Concept has very little in common with the ordinary concept. It is the dialectical Essence of Being having become aware or conscious of itself in human personalities. This concrete subject of thinking, which knows that it too, consciously, participates in the dialectical unity of all opposites and is the only reality which is intelligible in and for itself: Intelligibility exists, existence is intelligible. Hegel illustrates, for example, the Concept with Socrates: When Socrates says that it is not his sinews or muscles which explain why he does not want to escape from prison and death, but it is his understanding of the good which explains his actions, then this is a real personal existence which is intelligible in itself and for itself and for us. This is the Concept; it finds its concrete unity of subject and object, ideality and reality in many analogies in the natural and in the historical world. Therefore, while the ordinary idea of concept is fixed and rigid and maintains its identity in all its instances, Hegel's Concept constantly changes and modifies itself. Wherever there is an organic and living whole of many opposite aspects or polarities, conscious of itself, there the Concept dwells.

And now something strange happens. Once you get used to it and begin to understand this term, it is all of a sudden impossible to find any substitute for it, and so what seems to be perverse at the beginning becomes unavoidable at the end. Once you keep the distinction between the formal-logical concept and Hegel's Concept in mind, then you will be immune to the frequent misinterpretations of Hegel as a rationalist.

2. The second difficulty is his use of the philosophical genius of the German language. He uses root meanings of words forgotten in daily usage and loves to use words with multiple meanings.

One can know Kant without knowing German. His is a general, essentially Latin or scholastic terminology—whereas Hegel develops his language originally—one cannot know him without a mastery of German. This does not preclude translations into other languages—it is merely much more difficult. "Aufheben" means cancel, preserve and elevate in one word; "endlich" (finite) is that which "ends"; its destiny is "zu fallen" (to fall)—its category is "Zufall" (contingency). Finite things, "gehn zu grunde" (perish)—but in perishing, they realize that

3

their common "Grund" (ground) is beyond their immediacy. "*Vernunft*" (comprehension) is derived from "vernehmen"—to "take something in orally and make it your own," or "listening to" the voice of "spiritual" value-realities. "*Wesen*" (essence) belongs to the past participle (gewesen) of the verb "sein" (to be). Hegel translates here a very similar expression of Aristotle: "the what was being." "Begriff," "grasp" comes from "greifen"; "be-greifen" is grasp something all around, have it in one's grip. The Concept grasps and holds a totality of living functions within itself; the translation of "Geist" by "Mind" is too intellectualistic, by "Spirit," too special, "spiritualistic." "Meinung" (opinion) is "mine." "Zweifel" (doubt), "Verzweiflung" comes from "zwei"—"two"— it means falling apart, in "Verzweiflung (desperation), irredeemable: "Philosophy is the way of Zweifel and Verzweiflung." "Erinnerung"—"reminiscence" is also actively making a content your own—appropriating it "inwardly" making it "inner." "Gattung" in German means kind or genus; "Begattung" means copulation or pairing; so Hegel writes: The *Gattung* realizes its concreteness through the process of *Begattung*.

This rich and concrete use of German requires many more words and sentences in English to transscribe. I have put the German terms in parentheses, so that the reader can get used to the Hegelian glossary. On the negative side: *Verstand* is always "reason," not "understanding"; Vernunft is *never* "reason," but always comprehension. *Wirklich* is never "real," but always "actual."

3. The third difficulty is what I call Hegel's mask. The concrete and living thought simply disappears in a fog of abstractions.

In my Hegel book[*] I have shown how this mask

---

[*] Gustav Emil Muller: *Hegel. Denkgeschichte eines Lebendigen.* Bern. A Francke Verlag. 1959.

was forming during his student days in Tübingen. After being spoiled by the Greeks, he was exposed to Christian theology. He fiercely tore into the "New Testament" and the early church with a radicalism which is more thorough and detailed than Nietzsche's. He is shocked and disgusted—but cautiously hides his thoughts, so that his teachers were deceived.

This is the original root of an irony which becomes habitual. He constantly deprives words of their customary meaning—and then complains that he is not understood or misunderstood. His desire to be understood is in conflict with his desire to be hidden.

For example he says philosophy must be a *system:* But if you look closely, you find that system means the impossibility of any system; systematic philosophy is the thorough demolition of all and every system. His "system" is a chain-reaction of exploded systems and standpoints. Or, philosophy must be *Science:* If you examine this closely you find that it has no similarity to what we ordinarily would call science. What he means by Science is simply a logical maturity beyond any "isms," including "rationalism" or "absolute idealism." A case of "indirect communication" if there ever was one! "Recht" is understood as that, which is studied in law-schools; but not in Hegel! He stretches the term to cover all ethical problems whatsoever.

4. There is what I call his pseudo-dialectic or "speculative fallacy," "speculative" used in the ordinary derogatory sense. In flagrant violation of the precepts of his own *Logic*, which says that sciences proceed undialectically under the rules of formal-logical methods, he nevertheless interferes with their object-problems and "construes" their finite facts in a pseudo-dialectical terminology—which is as unscientific as it is unphilosophical! And, adding insult to injury, constantly quarrels with the scientific method for not following his speculative fallacies.

5

The translator must distinguish, therefore, between genuine dialectic as the logic of philosophy, and the spurious pseudo-dialectic misapplied to finite objects. I have, in parentheses, indicated where I detected and consequently omitted speculative fallacies from translation, because there is no sense in perpetuating rubbish. In my *Hegel* I have traced this unfortunate deviation from his own principles to the baneful influence which Schelling had over him in Jena. Almost all the pseudo-dialectical blunders in Hegel's philosophy of nature—which also contains sound and magnificent ideas—are almost entirely taken over from Schelling.

5. Finally there is confusion worse confounded.

Hegel desperately lashes out against his linguistic helplessness by using various external devices to make clear what is not clear.

Italics are used profusely and indiscriminately, so that they lose their proper function. I have therefore disregarded them and underline only a few key words in each paragraph. All italics in this edition are either mine or my selection. A sample of Hegel's use is preserved in a literal quotation in §252.

The second device is a mechanical division of the text by *number* and *letters:* A, B, C; A1, A2, A3; A1a, A1b, A1c, etc. Then again he reacts angrily against his own clumsiness and warns his reader that this formalism of letters and numbers is quite artificial and superficial, and should not be taken seriously. I have followed this advice and omitted all such distracting divisions. Their worst effect was to nourish and give a semblance of plausibility to the Hegel legend of "thesis-antithesis-synthesis."

Finally, he misleads the reader by choosing wrong titles. For example, the first categories in the *Logic* —Being, Nothing, Becoming, Existence—*should* read: Being, Negativity or Freedom, Origin, Omnipresence. (*Existence* is taken up in §81, *Becoming* in §201.)

Hegel smiles on his own weakness, hiding at the

same time behind an absurd "we Germans": "We are known as profound thinkers, who are, however, not infrequently unclear. We want to know the innermost nature of things and their necessary coherence; and, in philosophy, we go to work on it systematically —yet we lapse sometimes into a formalism of superficial and arbitrary constructions." (X. 86)

There are four editions of Hegel's *Encyclopedia of Philosophical Sciences*.

Basically I have followed the first edition of 1817, which is the briefest, but is often enigmatic in its brevity. The second edition of 1827 and the third of 1830 is one hundred paragraphs longer, containing some very valuable philosophical additions, which have been included in my text; where I have used both editions, I have added the corresponding § of the second edition in parenthesis. The fourth edition of 1840-1845 has been swelled to three formless volumes; the editors stuffed it with lecture notes from many students and from many semesters—there are, for example, around eighty pages discussing excerpts from a botany textbook! Occasionally I have used those footnotes when they contain clues as to what Hegel was talking about in the paragraphs; they are put in quotation marks, volumes and pages indicated.

Note: A complete account of all texts and later editions of the encyclopedia are found in the new critical edition in Meiner's Philosophische Bibliothek, 1959.

GEORG WILHELM FRIEDRICH HEGEL*

At this writing, one-hundred and twenty-eight years have elapsed since Hegel's death. What happened to his philosophy during this period?

His *philosophy of religion*** was vigorously developed by Bruno Bauer in his historical critique of the gospels: As history they are worthless. Christian Ferdinand Bauer showed the historical formation and transformation of the Christ-dogma. David Friedrich Strauss understood the construction of the gospels out of incompatible dogmatic requirements: Immanuel Biedermann and others interpreted the mythical language of various religions and theologies as symbolic representations of dialectical truth: The Absolute implies neither an impersonal pantheism, nor an abstract theism; God is neither one with the world, nor is he apart from the world.

Ludwig Feuerbach and Karl Marx completely miss this dialectic by making religion entirely subjective.

Hegel's discovery of the *history of philosophy* as gradual self-disclosure of world-itself, was carried out by Johann Edward Erdmann's monumental *His-*

---

* The numbers quoted refer to volumes and pages of *Hegel. Sämmtliche Werke.* Jubiläumsausgabe. Stuttgart. Fromann; the titles, covered by the numbers, are found in the Appendix.

** See my article: Die Entwicklung der Religionsphilosophie in der Hegelschen Schule. Zeitschrift für philosophische Forschung. 1950. Volume 3.

tory of Philosophy[1] which still is and probably always will remain the standard work in its field. Hegel's *Aesthetics,* likewise, which understood Beauty as the ontological interplay of opposites, imagined in the form of appearance, was pursued in Friedrich Theodor Vischer's equally monumental Aesthetics[2] in six volumes—which likewise has hardly been matched by anything in this philosophical discipline. Kuno Fischer's *Hegel* (1901) in two volumes is the clearest and most accurate reproduction and condensation of the contents of Hegel's works.

But the main impact of Hegel was negative. Kierkegaard wants to save his Christian soul from "the system"; Schopenhauer protests in the name of a blind, greedy, irrational will-to-live against a so-called rationalism and "ruthless optimism." To a host of long-bearded, progressive naturalists, Hegel is a confused, romantic dreamer, at best a "metaphysical poet." For Marx, he is too theoretical and not practical enough. For academic "epistemologists" he is too practical, too involved in the life of the world. In sum: he is attacked from the most incompatible and opposite extremes—his dialectic was too comprehensive for any radicalism. And today? Husserl's phenomenology and various existentialisms have merely paved the way to a deeper understanding of Hegel— the rebirth of his dialectic is reabsorbing them!

Who is Hegel? What is the essence of his vision and of his philosophical existence? What does he mean to us and our global century—so radically different from his Europe-centered world?

We start with the trite and obvious fact: Hegel is a *German* philosopher who lived between August 27,

---

1. Johann Edward Erdmann. *Versuch einer wissenschaftlichen Darstellung der Geschichte der neuern Philosophie.* New edition in seven volumes. Stuttgart. Frommann. 1932.

2. *Aesthetik oder Wissenschaft des Schönen.* 1846.

1770, and November 14, 1831, and spent his whole life in learning, writing, and teaching.

Under one of his portraits, he wrote: "Unsere Kenntnis soll Erkenntnis werden. Wer mich kennt, wird mich hier erkennen." Literally untranslatable, this passage means: A given fact with which we are familiar, both hides and reveals those living energies and their historical deeds and destinies of which the present fact is a result and an expression. What is given must be understood as a phase of its own becoming. Knowledge is a task (soll). And, finally, I am a task and problem to myself.

The cities he lived in, Stuttgart, Tübingen, Bern, Frankfurt, Jena, Bamberg, Nürnberg, Heidelberg, Berlin, are all centers of German culture, capitals of various German stock—Swabian, Alemannian, Franks, Prussians—they lie South and North, East and West —they are Protestant or Roman Catholic. Hegel is *essentially* German; he represents German culture no less than Goethe. What he describes as the good German character is also a self-portrait:

"And if we may brand any particular condition of soul-life as distinctively German, it is just this loyal, careful,[1] and good-natured citizenship, which in a self-respect that is without pride, in a piety which is not merely fanatic or bigoted, but is also at home in the world, remains neat and clean . . . he combines his own enduring sense of independence and advancing freedom with loyalty to its former moral customs, preserving the sterling character of his forefathers unimpaired."[2]

He implores his people to keep culture and the "holy flame" of philosophy as their sacred mission —like Jewish prophets implored Israel to keep faith-

---

1. Wohlhäbig—not Wohlhabend—one who takes good care of what he possesses.
2. XIV, 122.

ful to their national deity.[1] German and philosophical culture should form an indissoluble union.

Kant, by contrast, is a "world-citizen"—because he assumes "reason" to be everywhere the same. Hegel is world-filled. He is the philosopher of "World-itself." The concretenes of his German existence is the key to "see" other equally concrete cultural wholes in other times and places. His travels to Paris, the Netherlands, Vienna show his enthusiastic openness to the concrete genius of other cultures. The "Concept" is a universal value of life, existing in particular and individual differentiations; an existential act, realizing an essential structure of universal opposites united in a unique organic whole. These "Concepts," by opposing each other, constitute a dynamic, historical world. They "hang together" in spite of and through their differences; "if it were permissible to yearn for being something which we are not, the longing for classical Greece would be permissible. But it is not permissible." "Truth must be filled with historical life"[2]—and life is never "life in general."

Hegel's *historical time* spans the 18th century enlightenment of Leibniz, and of Kant and the romantic breaking of forms in a vision of the Infinite. The tremendous upheaval of the great French Revolution and the power of Napoleon were experienced by him as the political "actuality" analogous to the "comprehension" of freedom and self-activity in German philosophy. The subsequent reaction under Metternich was treated by Hegel with sarcastic irony. He remains anchored in the revolutionary age of his youth. "Given," "positive," traditional orders of life had to be examined and reconstituted as orders and embodi-

---

1. W. XVII, 20.
2. W. II, 161.

11

ments of a rational freedom, justifying the infinite dignity of man. "In Germany, this principle has burst forth as thought, spirit, self-knowledge (Begriff); in France, in the form of political actuality."[1] Whereas the French actualized freedom, not only in their own country, but also in Europe, the German on the contrary "quietly keeps his night-cap on."[2]

Hegel's philosophical personality unites the rational and sober interest in finite, concrete shapes of historical and cultural life (including factual sciences) with the infinite and tragic awareness of their limitations. "Philosophy demands the unity and intermingling of these two points of view: It unites the Sunday of life when man in humility renounces himself; and the working day, when he stands independently, is master of himself and considers his own interests."[3] But, unlike his romantic friends— Schelling, Hölderlin—he did not believe that the Absolute, the concrete and all-encompassing totality of cosmic and historical life, could be had, enjoyed, and thought directly, immediately as an eternal "thing-in-itself" apart from its temporal manifestations. The eternal Being is not a mere beyond; an indefinite future or a golden past; the goal of a vague longing. The Absolute reveals itself in limited, immediate, and always questionable shapes of life, which it also transcends, cancels, and yet preserves. The eternal, absolute, intelligible Being is one with this temporal, relative, experienced world of nature and of man.[4] This is the dialectical-ontological-cosmological-historical "comprehensive" truth (Vernunft) which Hegel first worked out in his early studies of the Christian religion—where Christ is a concrete past, a promised future, as well as an eternal present.

1. W. XIX, 535.
2. W. XIX, 553.
3. W. XVII, 126.
4. W. XIX, 118.

If you try to embrace the Absolute directly, immediately, intuitively, you embrace your own Nothing, the annihilation of your own limited perspective and merely subjective standpoint. That you gain your true self in losing it in the Absolute is a truth which all mystics have proclaimed—and in this sense Hegel calls his philosophy "mystic"—this annihilation of a finite as absolute is a "moment" of truth:[1] "When man begins to philosophize, the soul must commence by bathing in this ether of the One Substance, in which all that man has held as true has disappeared; this negation of all that is particular, to which every philosopher must have come, is the liberation of the mind and its absolute foundation."[2]

His term "Concept" (Begriff) was originally derived from Kant's "synthesis a priori" of logical form and non-logical, perceptual content—but enlarged beyond the realm of science. Kant's "synthesis a priori" becomes the dialectical unity of all opposites — a unity existing in the thinker in whom it becomes conscious for itself what is in in itself—this is the "Concept" of the philosopher involved and becoming aware of himself in all realms of reality. In Kant, true knowledge is restricted to the realm of science, philosophically comprehended as this "synthesis"—in Hegel this realm of empirical science is only one of the many forms of "spiritual" life, "world-shapes," in which World-itself becomes what it is; it must be thought, in order to make the absolute totality of all possible experience, which is not an experience, clear and articulate. The infinite and eternal totality of a living reality must be patiently produced and reproduced in its many dimensions. Hegel demands the utmost of patience; patient, laborious work is the imperative of philosophical existence, hoping to make itself conform to the patient and slow self-manifesta-

1. W. VIII, 198.
2. W. XIX, 376.

tion of World-itself. "In mentioning Plato's manner
. . . one is reminded of the tale, that he has reworked
his books on the State over seven times . . . such a
reminder . . . would prompt the desire to have been
granted for a work (the Logic) which, as belonging
to the modern world, has a more difficult problem
and a more complex and richer subject-matter to
master, the free leisure to work through it seven times
seventy times."[1] In Hegel, philosophy has matured,
has become professional, co-operative—this he calls
"scientific."

Philosophy is "Science," not merely feeling, intuition, belief—but what these "non-scientific" activities
have and are and create in living minds becomes the
non-logical value-content of logical-philosophical reflection. If there is no thinking in them, then they
merely happen—they come and go without universal
significance. "This philosophical comprehension (Vernunft) is the organ for all spiritual value-experi-
ences."[2] All philosophy is logical in form and more
than logical in dynamic value-content. The "Whole,"
which is the "Truth," is always this "together" of
rational and non-rational "moments"—this is "The
comprehending Concept" (Vernünftiger Begriff).
Historically speaking, Hegel is the synthesis of en-
lightenment-rationalism and romantic irrationalism.

"Philosophy is one's own time collected in the
form of thought."[3] This idea that philosophy is the
self-conscious expression of its own time has frequently been misinterpreted, as if Hegel meant a
passive acquiescence in some status quo. But when
Hegel says "time," he means its moving vanguard, as
expressed in his poem *Resolution*:[4]

Boldly the son of the gods entrusts his worth to
the battle.

1. W. IV, 34.
2. W. XIX, 547f.
3. W. VII, 35.
4. Dok., 388.

14

> Break then the peace with yourself, break with the
>   peace of the world!
> Strive! Attempt much more than today and yester-
>   day brought us.
> Better not than your time—but be time at its best.

The dead, reactionary echo of a past time he calls,
ironically, sound common sense (gesunder Menschen-
verstand). "What one calls sound common sense is
not philosophy—it is even often very unsound. The
sound common sense is a garbage-can of the maxims
of its time. For example, before Copernicus, it would
have been against all sound common sense, if some-
one had contended that the earth revolved around
the sun . . . sound common sense contains all the
prejudices and fashions of the time; it is governed by
them without being conscious of that fact. Philosophy transcends common sense."[1]

We have placed Hegel's life between 1770 and
1831; in turn, he has given meaning and cohesion to
this, his time . . . not only as a thinker, but also as
a pathetic, passionate victim, as well as an active
participant. Yet, he transcends his own existential
time and remains real and significant for us, his future; and again, his sense for the reality and importance of his own time is made the key to the equally
concrete *understanding of all other times*, which pre-
ceded his. This is meant, when he says man must
become "essential"—just as all Being transcends its
immediacy, which is nevertheless retained in its mediated "essence." "Wesen" means: Being is what it is,
together with its becoming, with its being conditioned by its "having-been" (gewesensein) and by
its anticipating a real future. Just like the fruit of a
plant is its immediate being now and is at the same
time made possible by the whole process of the
plant's life in all its phases.

"Spirit" (Geist) is existential time transcending

---

1. W. VIII, 36.

itself[1]; although it is embodied in particular "world-shapes" as well as in individual agents—although it is particularized and individualized, concrete and unique, nevertheless, it is not confined to national boundaries or historical relativity. As individual modification of a whole of life, it is also eternal; it does not drop out of the universe of Being which it helps to constitute and to express through its transition and finitude. The real past hangs together with the real present and the equally real future. "Immortality means that the human individual has an infinite value in and for itself; this is the principle of self-knowledge and freedom beyond the mortality of nature."[2] The dialectical process and structure of reality eternally IS—to participate in it—in agreement with it—is our immortal destiny.

"Men do not, at certain epochs, merely philosophize in general, for there is a definite philosophy which arises among a people; the definite character of the standpoint of thought permeates all other historical sides of the spirit of the people. The particular form of a philosophy is thus contemporaneous with a particular constitution of a people amongst whom it makes its appearance. With their institutions and forms of government, their morality, their social life and the capabilities, customs, and enjoyments of the same; it is so with their attempts and achievements in arts and sciences, with their religions, warfares, and external relationships; likewise with the decadence of the states in which this particular principle and form had maintained its supremacy, and with the origination and progress of new states in which a higher principle finds its manifestation and development. *Geist* in each case has elaborated and expanded in the whole domain of its manifold nature the principle of the particular stage of self-conscious-

---

1. W. IX, 82.
2. W. XII, 474, also W. XVII, 269.

16

ness to which it has attained. Thus, the Geist of a people in its richness is an organization, and, like a cathedral, is divided into numerous vaults, passages, pillars, and vestibules, all of which have proceeded out of one whole and are directed towards one end. Philosophy is one form of these many aspects. And which is it? Is it the fullest blossom, the "Concept" of Geist in its entire form, the consciousness and conscience of all things, the living reality of the time in connection with a temporal world present to itself. The multifarious whole is reflected in it as in the single focus, in the "Concept" which knows "himself" . . . this is the position of philosophy amongst its varying forms, from which it follows that it is entirely identical with its time. But if philosophy does not stand above its time in content, it does so in form, because, as the thought and knowledge of that which is the living value-content of its time, it makes that Geist its object."[1]

But as soon as this creative, streaming, productive life is objectified—as soon as the "spirit" steps back, reflects, looks back on its own achievements, it necessarily has transcended a given shape of life. What becomes an object of reflection is finite "and nothing finite is true or as it ought to be." The *Idea*—Hegel's term for teleological process—abolishes these finite forms. A philosophy, which has not the absolute form identical with the content, must pass away because its form is not that of truth"[2]—it is only a matter of a temporal "now" or "fashion." Truth is identical with the unfinality of all finite modifications of the One reality, which nevertheless IS in all and preserves, "remembers" (er-innern) them all.

In other words, each philosophy shall fill and fulfill its own time to its own level best, and yet must know the tragic essence of its own temporality. "No

---

1. W. XVII, 84-86.
2. W. XVII, 66.

philosophy has ever been refuted," because the Absolute is momentarily or immediately present in each; what is refuted "is not the principle of this philosophy, but the fact that this principle should be considered final and absolute."[1]

The eternal Being is one with its own restless and temporal Becoming. Its transcendence, its absolute unity, is only one "abstract" aspect of its totality. The personal, existential philosophizing necessarily must transcend itself to be itself and must identify itself with the absolute or non-relativistic historicity of philosophy.

How does Hegel see himself as a *philosophical personality?*

The "modern" philosopher, he says, knows himself in contrast to those "shapes" (gestalten) of philosophical existence in the past, which he had been, can no longer be, but which he also remembers and preserves. Speaking on philosophers in the modern world: "In respect to the *lives* of the philosophers, it will strike us that from this time on (Renaissance) these appear very different from those of the philosophers of ancient times; those self-sufficing individualities required that a philosopher should live as he teaches; this the ancients have accomplished. They are such *plastic individualities* just because the inward spiritual aim of philosophy has determined their appearance and position in society. The object of their knowledge was to take a thoughtful view of the universe; they kept the external world all the further removed from themselves, because they did not greatly approve of much therein present . . ." Hence with the Greeks and Romans the philosophers lived in an independent fashion peculiar to themselves, and in a mode of life which appeared suitable to and worthy of the science they professed.

In the Middle Ages it was chiefly the clergy, doc-

---

1. W. XVII, 67.

tors of theology, who occupied themselves with philosophy; as *monks* they renounced all temporal goods.

In the transition period the philosophers showed themselves to be in an inward *warfare with themselves* and in an external warfare with their surroundings, and their lives were spent in a wild, unsettled fashion.

In modern times things are very different; now we no longer see philosophic individuals who constitute a class by themselves . . . nor are they monks. We find them generally in connection with the world, participating with others in some common work or calling. They live, not independently, but as *citizens* they take part in the life of the state and occupy public offices. Certainly they may be private persons, but if so, their position as such does not isolate them from their other relationships. They too are involved in present conditions, in the world and its work and progress. . . . This difference is founded in the history of the modern world: After the building up of the inward world of religion, outward conditions have taken shape. In modern times . . . worldly life has become constituted and organized, in economic, legal, political systems, conformable to a reasonable nature. We see a universal, comprehensible *connection*, and with that individuality attains another character; it is no longer the plastic individuality of the ancients. This connection is of such power that every individuality is under its dominion; yet at the same time can build up for himself an inward world, so that both inward and outward may be self-sufficing and remain independent of one another. . . . With the higher degree of strength attained by the inward side of the individual, he may leave his external side . . . to be determined by the order which is present in the particular sphere in which his lot is cast. Life becomes scholarly, uniform, commonplace, it connects itself with outwardly given relationships, and cannot represent or set itself forth as a form pertaining only to itself. . . . A philosopher, it is said, should live as a philosopher, i.e., should be independent of the external relationships of the world, and should give up occupying himself with and troubling himself concerning them. But . . . no one can suffice for himself; he must seek to act in connection with others. The modern world is this essential power of connection, and it implies the fact that it is clearly necessary for the individual to enter into these relations of external existence. . . . The calling of philosophers is not, like that of the monks, an organized condition. Members of academies of learning are no doubt organized in part, but even a special calling like theirs sinks into the ordinary commonplace of state or class relationships, because admission thereinto is outwardly determined. *What really matters is to remain faithful to one's aims.*"[1]

This passage is a telling example of Hegel's irony: The simple-minded demand to "live" his philosophy is ridiculous to him—should he impersonate the Absolute? For his conception of the "modern" philosopher as a university professor or state-official, Hegel has been fiercely attacked and ridiculed by such "outsiders" as Schopenhauer and Kierkegaard . . . as if to be a teacher at a state university meant to be a slave of a political institution. Hegel knew the danger of a dead academic routine just as well as they. But he was determined to fill the ordinary and punctual life of a teacher with a most extraordinary freedom and courage of thought. "To be sleepy, merely to live, to be an official is not our essential Being; on the contrary: Not to be a slave."[2] He covered his intense and profound inward life with the protective mask of a prosaic professor and an ordinary "good-fellow," playing bridge.

Philosophy must be professional just as well as

1. W. XIX, 275-277.
2. W. XVII, 134.

jurisprudence or medicine, but its practice is education, the living dialogue between teacher and student together with the opportunity to keep abreast with professional literature as well as with its own history; this was Hegel's avowed purpose in founding his *Yearbooks for Scientific Critique.* A "modern" philosopher who would be a "plastic individuality" like Diogenes in his tub, a "sage" above the ordinary world; or a mystic visionary completely absorbed by religious concerns; or one confiding his private miseries to the market-place; or one seeking the "adventures of knight-errants"[1]—all such past shapes of philosophical existence would, if imitated or repeated, appear as comical anachronisms—although what they have accomplished is not lost from the spirit of philosophy. Actually, Hegel describes in these historical descriptions stations on his own life's road!

When the students honored him as their "great teacher," they had learned that Hegel was not merely a writer—all through his life, Hegel's educational-practical interests were just as strong and original as his theoretical-contemplative vision of the Absolute.

We have recalled Hegel in relation to his people and to other world-historical peoples; and in relation to his time and all historical times, and in his self-understanding. Before we take up the central question: What is the secret of his world-historical importance? Let us first dispose of his main weakness. His romantic friends called him "wooden," "leathery," or "pedantic"; but to positivistic, factual, or literal-minded people he appeared "deadly" or violently "constructive," "speculative" in the sense of not being true to factual experience. Alexander von Humboldt, for example, explorer and naturalist, professor of geography at the University of Berlin, says of his

1. W. XVII, 48.

colleague: "There is a forest of ideas in that Hegel, but for a man like myself, who is tied down to the earth and its natural differences, an abstract contention of facts, which is simply false, and his opinions about America and India, are oppressive and worrisome."[1]

This criticism touches Hegel's weakest point. Occasionally, he slips into that *speculative fallacy* which seems to absolutize mere factual knowledge or facts —as if the meaningless physical appearance of cosmic life could always be understood as a meaningful expression of that life—like a physical gesture of a person being understood as an expression of his real intention and action; or as if a blind mechanical causality were necessarily a willing instrument of intelligible ends or values—like a machine designed to serve higher ends. An example of his speculative fallacy: ". . . for the Christian this intelligible world had likewise this immediate sensuous truth of an ordinary course of events—a form which it must have and retain for the majority of men. This new world therefore *had to be* adopted by a new race of men, by barbarians; for it is characteristic of barbarians to apprehend the spiritual in a sensuous way. And it *must be* by northern barbarians, for it is the northern self-containedness alone that is the immediate principle of this new world-consciousness."[2] On the principles of his dialectic, however, the Absolute is just as present in the blindness of nature as in the visions of history. He is too inclined—against the precepts of his own logic—to construe factual sciences in pseudo-dialectical language and on the other hand, to call philosophy "Science"—what he means by that is logical maturity beyond "isms." But this ambiguous terminology has given rise to the legend that Hegel is a "rationalist."

1. Fischer, II, 1221.
2. W. XIX, 117.

And now to the positive question: What is his importance? It is, perhaps, easier to say what he is not. He is the critic of all extremists. Fanatics cannot survive in the medium of his dialectic. But fanatics can never understand a non-fanatic—what is not *for* them must be *against* them. The absence of extremes or one-sided "isms" appears as an even temper, as a harmonious balance, a reliable stability. But this again, is deceptive; his balance is not that of a "plastic shape," a classical statue—his thinking constantly moves in the most extreme "limiting situations," to use Jaspers' term. Every "Concept" meets its crisis and is forced to face its self-destruction. This is the skepticism which is one with every true philosophy. His balance is like the dynamic balance of a bicycle-rider.

What he says of *Geist* is true of himself: "But the world-spirit does not sink into this rest of indifference; this follows from its very nature, for its activity is its life. This activity presupposes a material already present, on which it acts, and which it does not merely augment by the addition of new matter, but completely fashions and transforms. Thus, that which each generation has produced in science and in intellectual activity is an heirloom to which all the past generations have added their savings; a temple in which all races of men thankfully and cheerfully deposit that which rendered aid to them through life, and which they had won from the depths of Nature and of Mind. To receive this inheritance is also to enter upon its use. It constitutes the soul of each successive generation, the intellectual substance of the time; its principles, prejudices, and possessions; and this legacy becomes a material, metamorphosed by *Geist*. In this manner that which is received is changed, and the material worked upon is both enriched and preserved at the same time.

This is the function of our own and of every age:

To grasp the knowledge which is already existing, to make it our own, and in so doing to develop it still further and to raise it to a higher level. In thus appropriating it to ourselves we make it into something different from what it was before. On the presupposition of an already existing intellectual world which is transformed in our appropriation of it, depends the fact that Philosophy can only arise in connection with previous Philosophy, from which of necessity it has arisen. The course of history does not show us the becoming of things foreign to us, but the becoming of ourselves and of our own knowledge."[1] As Goethe puts it:

But ye, God's sons in love and duty,
Enjoy the rich, the ever-living Beauty!
Creative Power, that works eternal schemes,
Clasp you in bonds of love, relaxing never,
And what in wavering apparition gleams
Fix in its place with thoughts that stand forever![2]

And: "It has been shown above in reference to the existence of Mind, (Geist) that its Being is its activity. Nature, on the contrary, is, as it is; its changes are thus only repetitions, and its movements take the form of a circle merely. To express this better, the activity of Mind is to show itself. I am, immediately, but this immediate "I am" is only a living organism; as Mind I am only in so far as I know myself, make myself my own problem. "Know thyself," the inscription over the temple of the oracle at Delphi, is the absolute command which is expressed by Mind in its essential character. But consciousness really implies that for myself, I am object to myself. In forming this absolute division between what is mine and myself, Mind constitutes its ex-

---

1. XVII, 29.
2. Faust. Prologue.

24

istence and establishes itself as external to itself. It postulates itself in the externality which is just the universal and the distinctive form of existence in Nature. But one of the forms of externality is Time, and this form requires to be further examined both in the Philosophy of Nature and the finite Mind.

Philosophy appears not only in thought but also as a progressive existence in time. Philosophy is thus the heart of history. "This progression is not one which takes its course only through the thought of an individual and exhibits itself in a single consciousness, for it shows itself to be universal Mind presenting itself in the history of the world in all the richness of its form."[1] Philosophy, then, is the moving critique of all one-sided "isms," abstract achievements which it produces, cancels, and preserves; it is the critique of institutions of life-in-action. It is, literally, a self-movement—the philosophizing self of mankind moves itself.

We illustrate this critical function of philosophy with a few one-sided "isms," which are dialectically cancelled, preserved, and integrated (aufgehoben). To mention them all would require a journey through the whole of Hegel's *Logic* and *Phenomenology*.

"*Rationalism* is opposed to philosophy in content and form."[2] The rationalist does not live the world as an existential problem; the problematic reality does not gain existence and dialectical self-knowledge in him. He merely knows intellectual riddles with guaranteed solutions. He says: "What I cannot think as true does not trouble me as doubt. A question which I do not understand, I cannot answer; it is for me as good as no question at all."[3] Such intellectualists are the very opposite of philosophical personali-

---

1. W. XVII, 61-62.
2. W. XVII, 112.
3. W. XIX, 537.

ties, because they are "self-satisfied, self-possessed, superior persons"[1]—literally, "obenauf"—irrepressibly superficial—like a cork always moves to the top of the water.

Reason, (Verstand) because it is abstract and general, and because its objects are selected and regional groups of finite appearances, misses reality altogether. It is like a "net" cast over—not reality, but over immediate objects and finite appearance over-against myself. "It is the net in which all concrete matter, which occupies mankind in action and impulses, is grasped. But this web and its knots in our ordinary consciousness only contains the objects and interest which we have over against us. A collection of facts known *about* this content is by its nature excluded from philosophy."[2]

Concrete, living development of Being in its individual and temporal shapes and in its self-consciousness is forever a mystery to reason.[3]

The rational-scientific method, philosophically understood, is itself one of the living shapes of Geist. But as long as the scientist is occupied with his finite objects, he is not aware of his own true existence. He rather thinks in terms of an additive, impersonal "progress," in which new facts are joining old facts. Philosophical contemplation or comprehension makes man's own activities, such as the rational-scientific, his own problem. "He (this Geist in the philosopher) takes his own self-estrangements back into himself as one with its own self-activity and existence. As concrete, this activity is a succession of processes in development which must be represented, not as a straight line drawn out into vague endlessness, but as a circle returning within itself,

1. W. XIX, 537.
2. W. XVII, 87, 88.
3. W. XVII, 112.

26

which, as periphery, has very many circles, and whose whole is a larger number of processes turning back within themselves."[1]

The vague progress into endlessness of object-sciences does not reach reality, because reality is already present at the beginning in the scientist as he separates himself from his object. Reality is equally present in both poles of this process, and the process, when it understands itself philosophically, realizes this. Process is real and reality is "in" this process. The changing borderlines of scientific knowledge are drawn within reality—they are at best only partly identical with Being.

Irrationalism is no less one-sided and undialectical than rationalism. The irrationalist sees that reality cannot be reached by abstract reason and so replaces it by irrational imagery, hunches, feelings, or super-rational myths. At best, it is the concrete Idea in a state of subconscious fermentation. "The irrational may be the beginning of the Comprehensive."[2] But it cannot express what it is or has, unless it *thinks* its own production in their universal human significance. It is like a dream, which may be very wise, which may represent the total situation of man in how he finds himself situated in reality—but unless the dream is remembered and expressed rationally in its universal meaning, it is not clear what we are or have in producing such dreams. At its worst, irrationalism becomes superstitious mythological pseudo-metaphysics.[3] Philosophy begins when man is free—that is, in agreement with himself—not when he is still in the clutches of alien demons or obsessions.

This brings us to another related pair of opposites,

1. W. XVII, 56.
2. W. VII, 279.
3. W. XVII, 96-100.

both of which are dialectically rejected and absorbed. One pole is *objectivism* or realism, the other, *subjectivism* or idealism.

The philosopher becomes concrete and existential, when he resolutely dedicates all he is and has to the one all-absorbing task of making reality explicit. World-itself is to become articulate. There is nothing arbitrary or subjectivistic in this task. But what reality is in itself must never be confused with object-thinking, which thinks that which is given to me, as "an other" totally alien to myself; the "other" and "I" together express a total and real situation. Mere "erudition is, in the main, acquaintance with a number of useless things, which have no intrinsic interest or value further than being known."[1] In objectivism man has lost himself. Mere objectivity, which confuses a given object with reality, is the principle of all "positivism," and authoritarian acceptance of contents on blind faith. "Self-thinking is held in bounds by faith and blind authority."[2]

But in subjectivism man loses himself just as much:

"If the history of Philosophy merely represented various *opinions* in array, whether they be of God or of natural and spiritual things existent, it would be a most superfluous and tiresome science, no matter what advantage might be brought forward as derived from such thought-activity and learning. What can be more useless than to learn a string of bald opinions, and what more unimportant? Literary works, being histories of philosophy in the sense that they produce and treat the ideas of Philosophy as if they were opinions, need be only superficially glanced at to find how dry and destitute of interest everything about them is.

An opinion is a subjective conception, an uncon-

---

1. W. XVII, 39.
2. W. XVII, 41.

28

trolled thought, an idea which may occur to me in one direction or in another: An opinion (Meinung) is mine, it is not in itself a universal thought which is existent in and for itself. But Philosophy possesses no opinions; there is no such thing as philosophical opinions. When we hear a man speaking of philosophical opinions, even though he be an historian of philosophy, we detect at once this want of fundamental education. Philosophy is the objective science of truth . . . and neither opinion nor the spinning out of opinions."[1]

On the other hand, the subject and his own insight and conviction is just as essential to philosophy as is its ontological orientation. "It is true that personal conviction is the ultimate, absolute, and essential, which comprehension or philosophy demands of the subject in knowledge."[2]

But just as reality in itself must not be confused with given and appearing objects, just so must the essential and inner subject of philosophy not be confused with mere psychical "points of view" or perspectives. ". . . when Christ said, 'I came into the world that I should bear witness unto the Truth,' Pilate answered, 'What is Truth?' That was said in a superior way, and signifies that this idea of truth is an expedient which is obsolete: We have got further, we know that there is no longer any question about knowing that Truth, seeing that we have gone beyond it. Who makes this statement has gone beyond it indeed. If this is made our starting point in the history of philosophy, its whole significance will consist in finding out the particular ideas of others, each one of which is different from the other: These individual points of view are thus foreign to me; my thinking reason is not free, nor is it present in them: For me they are but extraneous, dead his-

---

1. W. XVII, 40.
2. W. XVII, 42.

toric matter, or so much empty content, and to satisfy oneself with empty vanity is mere subjective vanity itself."[1]

The dialectical philosopher must neither lose himself in given objects, nor must he indulge in the illusion, vanity and hypocrisy, that he knows it all better and that he has advanced beyond all real and objective values of the world. He must so incorporate them in himself, that his true and independent self *becomes* for itself. Reality is thus both "in and for itself," and its eternal values are present in the mortal finitudes, to which they impart meaning and happiness—the "concrete moment."

These few examples may suffice to illustrate Hegel's dialectic. Man becomes truly human, man becomes himself and gains his own existence in a never-ending battle of opposites, to which he gives himself. "I am this battle, this living opposition in which the opposites are not external to one another, but are inseparably linked. I am not only one of the fighters, but I am both and I am also the battle itself."[2]

The philosopher is a dialectical movement in which he becomes what he is. If we again look back on Hegel's development we see a perfect realization of this "Concept" he is already what he will be in his first reflections, his constancy is just as evident, as his untiring effort at self-expansion.

But the individual philosopher, the "existing Concept" is only "abstract" by and for himself. He is a small sample of humanity in its historical self-realization. More than that: The dialectical structure which he knows himself to be, this self-knowledge which he is, can only "find itself in producing itself; it thus

---

1. W. XV, 80.
2. W. XV, 80.

only exists and is actual in finding itself."[1] This free activity of thought which is one with the core of philosophical-human existence is also the key to disclose the dialectical structure of Being itself on all its levels of self-manifestation. "What the history of philosophy shows us is a succession of noble minds, a gallery of heroes of thinking comprehension, who by the power of this comprehension have penetrated the being of all things, of nature and of spirit and the essence of God, and have won for us by their labors, the highest treasure, the treasure of comprehensive wisdom."[2]

In short, the "living Concept" or existing individual philosopher is incomprehensible apart from the "absolute Idea"—the dialectical life of the whole. *Dialectic* is the answer to the question: What is Hegel's world-historical significance.

There are many beginnings of Hegel's philosophy. It begins all at once with an incredible universality of interests and concerns. His philosophy is the logical reflection on *all* essential values of human existence in reality—including intense personal-moral problems, or political worries; his *systematic philosophy* unfolds all those values in their mutual, dialectical interrelation; in each of them there are, furthermore, levels or degrees ascending from lower to higher (See the logical diagram in Appendix).

Ivan Ilyin's magnificent work on *Hegel's Philosophy as Contemplative Theology* has singled out and over-emphasized religion as *one* beginning; it has shown, nevertheless, that this philosophy must remain incomprehensible, as long as the reader does not also "see" the religious act or vision, which becomes articulate in dialectical-logical reflection. From

---

1. W. XVII, 31.
2. W. XVII, 27.

31

his early wrestling with the Jewish and Christian texts and creeds to his last lectures on the Proofs of the Existence of God, always there is this religious concern, which binds together and dominates the whole of his philosophizing.

"God has condemned me to be a philosopher," is a sigh his wife frequently heard, as she told friend Niethammer after Hegel's death. It has been the same meaning as when the prophets complained of the burden which God's voice laid upon them.

Again, as usual, Hegel never speaks of his own religious experience, although he was thoroughly familiar with the mystics, particularly with Meister Eckhardt, where such descriptions abound; nor do we find any confessions endorsing any particular creed. "Philosophy must avoid the intention or will to be edifying"—because it *is* already "edified"— Truth and Being are in need of no propaganda. The intensity and power of Hegel's religious act is so pure, that it can neither find or express itself in "positive" religions nor in a special philosophy of religion. It permeates the whole existence and is the infinite background for the dialectical vision of the created world. The dialectical relation of the Absolute as infinite, perfect, and holy Being to the finite and always imperfect human existence is the "absolute Geist"—which is the ultimate and all-embracing formula for Hegel's philosophy as a whole.

This religious dialectic moves between the poles of finite desperation and infinite consolation. In Christian language between the message of Good Friday: "God is dead . . . my God, why hast Thou forsaken me"—and the Easter mesage: "I and the Father are one." The Holy One appears both in the "Nothing" of all finite beings, if they try to assert their own being in and for themselves, which is alienation from God, sin and evil—as well as in absolute unity of Being unconditionally present in all transitory and conditioned beings. Every step and

phase of Hegel's Logic is a modification and varia-
tion of this dialectic of finite and infinite, immediate
and mediated, absolute and relative, unconditional
and conditional, eternal truth and inevitable experiential error.

"These are the abstract propositions regarding
the nature of the Idea and of its development, and
thus within it Philosophy in its developed state is
constituted: It is one Idea in its totality and in all its
individual parts, like one life in a living being, one
pulse throbs throughout all its members. All the
parts represented in it, and their systematization,
emanate from the one Idea; all these particulars are
but the mirrors and copies of this one life, and have
their actuality only in this unity. Their differences
and their various qualities are only the expression of
the Idea and the forms contained within it. Thus the
Idea is the central point, which is also the periphery,
the source of light, which in all its expansion does
not come without itself, but remains present and
immanent within itself . . . its own necessity also
constitutes its freedom."[1]

"I can ask nothing of you but to bring with you,
above all, a trust in Science and a trust in yourselves.
The love of truth, faith in the power of mind, is the
first condition of Philosophy. Man, because he is
Geist, should and must deem himself worthy of the
highest; he cannot think too highly of the greatness
and the power of his mind, and, with this belief, nothing will be so difficult and hard that it will not reveal
itself to him. The Being of the universe, at first hidden and concealed, has no power which can offer
resistance to the search for knowledge; it has to lay
itself open before the seeker—to set before his eyes
and give for his enjoyment, its riches and its depths."[2]

This is the "Easter" mood. The opposite mood,

---

1. W. XVII, 57.
2. W. XVII, 22.

expressing estrangement and crisis as condition of philosophy is stated as follows:

"It may be said that Philosophy first commences when a race for the most part has left its concrete life, when separation and change of class have begun, and the people approach toward their fall; when a gulf has arisen between inward strivings and external reality, and the old forms of religion, etc., are no longer satisfying; when Geist manifests indifference to its living existence or rests unsatisfied therein, and moral life becomes dissolved. Then it is that Geist takes refuge in the clear space of thought to create for itself a kingdom of thought in opposition to the world of actuality, and Philosophy is the reconciliation following upon the destruction of that real world which thought has begun."[1]

Experience is always questionable and problematic. It is utopian and a mere dream to expect it ever to be otherwise. The philosopher must not be a dreamer, caught in his own beautiful or "edifying" constructions. Philosophy must face the world and its problematic actuality. Not to struggle with it and to say what IS would be an "escape-philosophizing of incompetence" (Ohnmacht).[2]

From the notes of the Frankfurt period we know how personal, how lived, how existential this objective statement is—or how objectively Hegel sees his own philosophizing in the world.

Man philosophizes because he is in trouble. And he is always in trouble. He is always longing for self-integration and harmony, in the light of which ideals he feels their lack in his finite situation. "The finite is neither true nor ever as it ought to be."[3] Its trouble belongs to its existence, it is a self-created

---

1. W. XVII, 82.
2. W. XVII, 78.
3. W. XVII, 66.

34

trouble, a necessary process in which the achievement and the good of yesterday becomes a fixation to be overcome, an enemy of the good today. This is an essential and perennial situation, which no pragmatism can remove or do away with. But in the light of the Absolute, this is as it eternally ought to be. The "cross" of the problematic finite existence is eternally willed and reconciled in the infinite and holy Being and will of God. This, at any rate, is Hegel's understanding of the meaning of the Christian religion. And because this is its meaning, Hegel sees in it the realization of the "absolute religion." The "absolute Geist" is a "mysterium tremendum" as well as "fascinosum."

"A great man is one who forces others to interpret him."[1] The nineteenth century protected its own philosophical smallness against Hegel by embalming him in "thesis, antithesis, and synthesis."[2]

The Hegel renaissance of this century has rediscovered that Hegel is as infinite and baffling as reality itself—that all "isms," including "absolute idealism" become ridiculous when applied to him.

In my translator's note, I pointed to the difficulties of Hegel's abominable style. Now, I should like to praise its power and beauty.

Hegel is not only the world's worst stylist, but also one of the greatest masters of the art of words. Sometimes the length of his periods is the natural expression of masses of thought, developed and held together in a concrete unity.

His dense paragraphs in the *Logic* and the *Encyclopedia* are the result of laborious care—to find the most concentrated logical shorthand formula

---

1. Quoted by Ilyin without reference.
2. cf. My article: The Hegel legend of "thesis, antithesis, and synthesis." Journal of the History of Ideas. New York. 1958. vol. XIX. No. 3. Appendix.

for long studies of complex matters. Once one penetrates the fog of clumsy abstractions, the beauty and range of crystal-clear thought is breathtaking.

Several times I had this experience: I had studied together with a semester's seminar such topics as What is Time? What is the relation of Being and Becoming? or, of Appearance and Reality? or, The One and the Many—chapters of my book *The Interplay of Opposites**—and then, after many books and many discussions, looking up one or two short Hegel paragraphs—I found everything there, in most precise exactness—where before I did not understand a word and thought Hegel was writing gibberish.

No other philosopher has so many substantial insights expressed in unforgettable and flash-like pithy sayings.

This power of revelatory words is rooted in Hegel's intuitive thinking. He does not say what he has not "seen." There is nothing in the invisible reality of the soul which has not been turned outward in unfailing language; and concrete, objectified "shapes" of history are penetrated as expressions of inner intentions. With all his objectivity, he is always himself—never second-hand.

Hegel's style changes like the colors in the sea. In his letters he is easygoing, informal, enjoying his absent company; in his newspaper chats and in his letters to his artistic friends he is light, witty, charming; as critic he is thorough but benevolent and kind to the author criticized; but when he is out to defend himself against an enemy he is ruthless, crushing, and bitterly sarcastic; in the history of political writing he ranks with the best publicists; when he deals with the dialectic of "Being" he is reminiscent of the monumental simplicity of the early Greeks, in the logic of Essence he comes close to the subtle style

---

* Gustav E. Mueller: *The Interplay of Opposites. A Dialectical Ontology.* New York, Bookman Associates, 1956.

of Plato and Aristotle; while in the last parts of his Logic, dealing with the subject-logic, called the Concept—his style is as original as his ideas. In his religious writing he finds the tone of great prophetic and mystic writers; as ethicist, he is as conscientious and stern as the moral law; as aesthetician, the reader feels that there is real enjoyment of the arts and not only "theory" about them. To repeat: Hegel is one of the worst as well as one of the greatest stylists in philosophy.

Philosophy as a mode and expression of existence is as inseparable from artistic creation and enjoyment, as it is from participation in the problems of practical life or the scientific life which is all out for conquering the object-appearances of the world, as it is from the religious act of acknowledging and worshipping the presence of the Holy. Philosophy in Hegel's sense is never and least of all merely a matter of the intellect or reason. His keen enjoyment of great art and his appreciation of aesthetic-festive life is another important origin of his philosophizing.

Art is the sister Muse of this philosophy. Beauty is the enjoyment of the Absolute in the form of a sensuous presence. Life shines through sensuous surfaces; all its levels and problems are collected and transfigured in the symbolic form of wholeness and perfection: "Art . . . thinking imagination . . . mediates this consciousness."[1]

This is also a description of the fascination of Hegel's own philosophical style: through the sober, accurate grasp of concrete and particular manifestations of living reality always "shines through" the absolute One and Whole, the "abyss of annihilation," whose imperfect manifestations they are. The negation of finite forms is the true affirmation of the absolute form.

---

1. W. XVII, 101.

Again Goethe comes to mind. Both are writers of the world. In Goethe's infinitely rich existence Hegel is only a "moment"; but in Hegel's infinitely rich world, Goethe also takes a modest place within the wealth of art and literature spread out in Hegel's lectures on Aesthetics—which in turn are but one of the "circles" within the infinite "circle" of reality, where every "moment" is an immediate presence, a mediated result of a mediating beginning.

Hegel's favorites in literature—besides Goethe and Schiller—are the polarities of tragic and comic art in the Attic theater and in Shakespeare.

Tragic in the Greek plays is the absolute dedication of man to an ideal, which involves him necessarily with the obstreperous mediocrity of the world, inflicts suffering and punishment on him, who has dared to challenge it and who is willing to pay this price for his daring. This is the way Plato portrayed his Socrates. In Shakespeare, on the other hand, an achieved and harmonious state of affairs cannot be maintained and is ruined by inordinate ambition, restoring itself through the suffering and punishment of the guilty.

Comic, on the other hand, is the finitude of man, when he tries to cling to it as if it were his true reality. Hegel loves Aristophanes, on whose stage everybody is so immensely foolish in his narrow and private perspective, that everything must necessarily go to pieces.

This interpenetration of the tragic and the comic style, reflecting in the sensuous medium of art the dialectic of the infinite and finite—is also Hegel's style. That every "moment" takes itself seriously and is taken seriously by philosophy, is at the same time its tragi-comical irony, unknown to itself but known to "us," the phenomenologists of Geist, who are sitting both in the audience and are also acting on the stage. Hegel enjoyed the painful foolishness of his own contemporaries, even where he had to suffer under them.

There are good reasons for the *Hegel renaissance* in the twentieth century. The so-called breakdown of Hegel's "system" signalized the breakdown of human and philosophical culture, whose bitter fruits we have harvested in this century. Hegel requires an "informed consciousness" (gebildetes Bewusst-sein) which is just what was slipping away from us.

The extremes which he saw and integrated in himself have become more extreme; they flew apart in all directions, everyone of them in outcries of derision and contempt against Hegel.

And empty, analytic formalism and intellectualism, devoid of all reality-sense, stands against various forms of irrational immediacies and vitalisms; a dogmatic and moralistic finitism and impatient pragmatic secularism fights against a revived confessionalistic religious fanaticism and dogmatism; and uncritical scientism and technicism which confuses progress in physical machinery with human progress is opposed by a desperate "existentialism"—the voice of despairing, isolated souls—lost in mechanical mass-formations and abstractions; the loss of confidence of man in himself, the loss of his human dignity has its counterpart in dead and meaningless routines: The drifting aimlessness calls for coercion and totalitarian panaceas.

The name of Hegel in this situation is a sign of courage and wisdom, of hope and faith and love— the reaffirmation of an eternal humanism, collected in logical self-comprehension.

Philosophy heals at least that corruption of the world which reason has brought about.[1]

---

1. W. XVII, 82.

FOUR INTRODUCTIONS

LIBERAL EDUCATION:
PREPARATION FOR PHILOSOPHY

(In the year 1806 Napoleon defeated the Prussian army in the battle of Jena. Hegel, at that time professor of philosophy at the University of Jena, interrupted his writing—he was just finishing the last pages of the Phaenomenology of Mind—in order to watch from his window the French conqueror riding on his white horse into the surrendered town. Hegel had to give up his position (the University having next to no money) and become a newspaper editor in Bamberg. Two years later his friend Immanuel Niethammer, Bavarian minister of education, rescued him from journalism. He was appointed director of a humanistic Gymnasium in Nuremberg, which he was to modernize. He filled this administrative post from 1808-1816. Besides he taught some classes of elementary introduction to philosophy for his high school students, and worked on his second major work, the *Logic* which appeared in 1816 and brought him the call to the University of Heidelberg. As director he gave five addresses, one each year, on graduation day. These addresses together with his *Philosophische Propädeutik* for his high school students now form the third volume of his works.*

---

* *Sammtliche Werke III: Philosophische Propädeutik, Gymnasialreden und Gutachten über den philosophischen Unterricht, Stuttgart,* 1829.

Reprinted with permission from Educational Theory, Vol. V, No. 4, October, 1955, where it appeared under the title: *Hegel on the Values of Humanistic Educaiton.*

Those simple speeches as well as the confidential reports and advices to Niethammer are not only a beautiful, human, personal document, but also a classical statement on the educational values of humanistic education. I report:

"We are living in the midst of an immense historical crisis. Being occupied we are deprived of our own independent public life. We are threatened with hopelessness and indifference, evils of the soul which are greater than the sight of ruins and the corpses of cities. Under such circumstances it is elevating to observe the enthusiastic response with which the citizens rally around the great project of saving and renewing our educational institution.[1] (264)

Rightly so, for it is the young generation who must be prepared to meet the challenge of the new situation. What has gone is gone irrevocably. It is vain to miss it or to wish it back. What is old is not preferable, because it was adequate or perfect for its own time. The young generation must not be troubled through futile regrets and fond memories; it must be prepared to shoulder the new tasks and to make itself worthy of a happiness in the new world of the future. It is up to them that good things may come out of many years of troubles and deprivations.[2] (297) This new life, however, would not be possible if we would succumb to the temptation to take too seriously the ups and downs, the external successes and diversions of the world-show. To orient our youth merely in the momentary and transitory changes of the world would give them a false concept of the value of things.[3] (296)

Have we not recently seen that states which neglected or even despise to cultivate such an inner core of the soul in their members and only trained

---

1. III, 264.
2. III, 297.
3. III, 296.

them to mere utility, degrading the spirit to the function of a mere means, were caught in dangers without fortitude, and were brought low in the midst of plenty of their useful supplies?[1] (238)

The Function of the School

Having thus firmly sized up the historical situation, Hegel then turns towards the function of the school in this situation:

The school is a transition from the life in the family to the life in public; and it mediates between the past achievement of mankind and its hoped-for future. From the point of view of the pupil, schooltime is the time of growth, learning, expansion, progression; from the point of view of the educator, schooltime is the time of recurrent cycles of learning and of generations; from the point of view of itself, its temporal interest is to endure as an ideal whole throughout the slow changes of historical times.[2] (281) Education cannot understand itself merely as an experiment.[3] (232)

The life in the family consists of personal, private relations. The family relates through love, feeling, natural piety and mutual confidence. This relation is not an objective bond of common causes, but a natural bond of blood. The child is recognized here because it is the child of the family. It meets the love of its parents without merit and has to stand their tempers without recourse to right.

In public life, on the contrary, a man has validity through that which he is, does and represents; he has value only insofar as he has earned it. He is receiving little out of love or for love's sake. His cause, which he represents, not his private personality, is

---

1. III, 238.
2. III, 281.
3. III, 232.

that which makes him valuable. Public life goes on independent of his peculiar subjectivity, and he has to make himself fit to enter one of its many objective spheres of activity. His whole personality becomes an organ of his calling.

The school, then in order to effect this transition from private to public existence, separates the adolescent from his immediate family background. Education leads the child from the life of feeling and restricting needs to the freedom of thought and of intellectual self-activity. Learning strengthens his power to become master over immediate impressions and shifting externalities.[1] (268-269)

On the one hand, the school still continues in tendering personal-individual guidance and care; on the other hand, it already prefigures the public, adult world of serious activities. The pupil gets used to strangers as equals in a competitive game of competitive efforts.[2] (272-273) The feeling of the child's dependence is changed gradually to a feeling of self-activity, integrity and independence. This is brought about not through external discipline or obedience, but through the means of personal interest and love in connection with the joy of objective learning.[3] (271)

Hegel's New Latin School

(The school which Hegel was instrumental in transforming was an institution for the teaching of Latin and Greek. The new curriculum contained besides Latin and Greek, mathematical and physical sciences, history, modern German literature and three introductory courses in philosophy taught in three

1. III, 268-269.
2. III, 272-273.
3. III, 271.

46

successive semesters by Herr Direktor Hegel himself.)

Hegel says: "The old type of Latin school had its justification in a time when the ancient languages were the only means to acquire culture, and where practical skills could be picked up in practical life itself. This separation of life and culture was most unfortunate (unselig); but now there is an equally extremist tendency to do away with classical culture altogether; it is said that a people cannot call itself cultured which is not able to express the treasures of knowledge in its own language; the intimate mastery which we enjoy of our own language is lacking in any other which is merely acquired. But against this criticism, true as far as it goes, must be said that it contains the danger of triviality, since practical everyday experiences do not contain the power of cultivating and elevating the mind. We must, therefore, distinguish: There must be a general education, enabling every member of the people to learn things which are essential to us all as human beings, as well as special skills; but there remains and persists nevertheless a higher education for those who will be scholars in the true and ancient sense of the word. And they too have a right to receive an education proper to their high calling.[1] (234-236)

For two thousand years, European culture has grown in the soil prepared by Greece and Rome. And each renaissance of Western humanity was connected with a new and deeper understanding and fertilization by principles discovered in our own beginnings. It would be a suicidal, a disastrous superficiality, if we were to surrender to the utilitarian educators, who think that humanistic education is superfluous because its fruits are not immediately convertible into cash. The humanistic education in

---

1. III, 234-236.

its reformed and new organization must be preserved. Any true form must preserve, as well as transform, the principle of its own former self.[1] (232-234)

The differentiation of higher education in various branches, and the differentiation of scholarly education in the departments of classical languages, history, literature, and philosophy is, compared with the undifferentiation of older forms, a spiritual progress. For the nature of the spirit, and spiritual freedom is realized when it is present in different forms (departments) of its own organization, each form representing completely the same goal from its own point of view; thus each of the contributing departments can do its own work wholeheartedly because each knows that it is a moment of the whole, is in and for it as necessary as the other departments. Only that which concentrates itself around its own principle can become a consistent, definite something; the whole which it wholly represents thus gains depth through the fertile possibility of a many-faceted expertness. Continuity of the whole process and perfection in each phase is opposed to a bargain-counter variety of many things ending in mastery of nothing.[2] (236)

This passage is very instructive. It clearly shows what Hegel means when he says spirit or freedom. Spirit rests on the freedom where each department may pursue its own interests according to the law of its own concerns; freedom, conversely, rests on an idea of organic wholeness which differentiates itself but which holds its differentiated departments together in a protective unity.

The Values of Classical Studies

"That culture, arts and sciences of a people should stand on their own, then, does not imply that the

---

1. III, 232-234.
2. III, 236.

study of the Greeks and Romans are merely learned antiquarian curiosities good for an idle few.[1] (236), nor playthings for children. We are not merely inspecting a nursery when we come to grips with the "ancients." There are values in those original and founding cultures of Europe, which it would be perilous for us to bypass.[2] (236)

I believe I do not contend too much if I say that one who has not known the works of the ancients has lived without knowing perfection and beauty (237). If we care for perfection, therefore, the study of the Greeks primarily, and then of the Romans, must remain a foundation.[3] (237) The soul imbibes from their glorious masterworks an unforgettable flair of taste and reason, a profane baptism, as it were. But to be truly initiated into this mystery, external "survey courses" or general acquaintance is insufficient. We must take up room and board with them to absorb their atmosphere, their ideas and manners, even their errors and prejudices, in order to become citizens of their world—the most beautiful that ever existed. If the first paradise was a paradise of natural man, then this second and higher paradise was that of the human mind, which steps forth here in its finer naturalness, freedom, depth and serenity, like the bride out of the bridal chamber . . . but this serenity is not a childlike play, but is spread over a melancholy (Wehmut) which knows the hardness of destiny, but nevertheless is not beaten by it but maintains its freedom and its dignity. . . If we make ourselves at home in this element, all the faculties of our soul are stimulated, developed and trained, and in appropriating it we are enriched and become substantially improved.[4] (237)

Formal training is not indifferent to the content

---

1. III, 236.
2. III, 236.
3. III, 237.
4. III, 237.

... the content, when it is grasped by the soul, must not be only an occasion to develop formal powers and faculties, but it must be at the same time its nourishment. Sensuous and useful stuff, given in immediate experience, does not have this evocative value. Only a spiritual content which has value and interest in itself, can strengthen the soul and give it that inner independence, that substantial fortitude, which is the matrix of a wakeful, attentive openness and self-control. Only this spiritual core of absolute meaning and independent value of life can serve as a foundation for everything useful and reliable in all walks of life. . . . This spiritual nutrition in the most noble form, golden apples in silver bowls, are offered us in the works of the ancients, incomparable to those of other nations and periods. I merely remind you of the grandeur of their attitudes, their plastic excellence and patriotic virtue, which is free from repressive moralistic ambiguity; of the great style of their deeds and characters; of the rich variety of their experience, manners and constitutions—to justify the proposition that no other culture unites so much that is admirable, original and many-sided. So much for content or "substance"; it is inseparable from form.

But this wealth is tied up with language: Translations are like artificial roses without the tenderness, loveliness and softness of life; or like stale wine. Language is a musical soul, the element of inwardness, which disappears in imitations"[1] (237-239) The study of language has both a moral and a logical value. Progressive education (*fortschreitende Bildung*) is not a natural process, in which one cell is added to another . . . but cultural education must make its own previous self or achievement into a resistance, which it belabors and re-forms. The world of antiquity is not only something which we

1. III, 237.

acquire to possess, but also that in working with which, in contrast to which, we become what we are. Anything natural or spiritual, to become an object of our labors, must stand over against us, must have the appearance of estrangement or alienation. In the immediate world of feeling such an estrangement is felt as unhappiness—unhappy he who is estranged and torn away from that which his heart (*Gemüt*) held dear, venerable, unquestionable and sacred. This pain and sorrow of the heart, however, is inevitable in life, but softened and sublimated in that education which requires us to occupy our memory and our thought with a mediated and strange world. . . . And this is precisely what youth intensely desires for its own good. There is an inevitable illusion in youth that happiness must be sought elsewhere. It desires to escape its familiar and immediate environment and to find fulfillment in a wider horizon. . . . The depth and power which we attain is measured by the expanse into which we have dared to adventure, and by the energy by which we find and maintain our center to which we return. The self thus restored is a hardened, an experienced, an enriched and proved self. To find ourself by losing ourself is the universal nature of the spirit.[1] (240-241)

This is the moral or spiritual meaning of learning a language immediately not our own. The logical value is equally great: grammatical rules in abstraction or isolation are a lifeless mechanism. Mechanism is a necessary aspect of the mind, but the whole and living mind has the task to digest it and make it a free and mastered side of its life. The mastery of grammar is thus the beginning of logical thinking. In the grammatical structure of languages the intellect deposits its forms or categories, through which it makes the life of the world articulate. The mind, in studying them in their linguistic sound and expres-

---

1. III, 240-241.

sion, becomes intuitively (*anschaulich*) acquainted with its own functions. What the mind immediately or potentially is becomes its conscious possession.

In learning to master the grammatical rules of the ancient languages we are forced to think, whether we want to or not. We do not have the immediate habit, which brings about the right word-order without reflection in our own mother-tongue. In an alien language we must consciously reflect on the meaning of the different parts and particles of the sentences and must remember the rules to fit them correctly. This thinking constantly practices the logical method of subsuming the particulars under universals, and of analyzing parts in meaningful wholes. Thus reason becomes a second and trained nature in us.[1] (241-243)

The danger of this training is that it gets stuck in the abstract and dead mechanism of a mechanical intellect or in a mere word splitting without intuition or philosophy.[2]

Done right, however, young people enter their profession with an indestructible sanctuary in their souls. In our modern world of practical specializations and complexities it is more necessary than ever that we have a concrete comprehension of life as organic whole. Untrained and undisciplined, the ideals of youth are measureless. They lose themselves in a vague and bad infinity of demands and expectations, in the light of which they find the present sad and unsatisfactory. Humanistic education teaches them to find wholeness and perfection in measure and limitation. And all real achievement and greatness needs concentration and concrete unity. As men we are based on an infinite and ideal ground but we are also mortal and finite. If we create in ourselves the comprehension of a concrete and perfect whole of

---

1. III, 241-243.
2. III (Letter to Niethammer, Oct. 22, 1812, p. 302).

life, we are calmly fortified both against losing ourselves in merely finite particularities and excitement
of the moment as well as against a deedless and
pointless longing for utopias, a bad and abstract infinity. We have a spiritual home in the world.[1]
(286-287)

---

1. III, 286-287.

PREFACE OF THE FIRST EDITION OF THE ENCYCLOPEDIA (1817)

The need of my students has prompted me to bring into daylight, earlier than I had originally intended, this outline of my lectures on the entire scope of philosophy. The nature of a survey excludes detailed treatment of contents; it also minimizes their systematic justification or proof, so indispensable in scientific philosophy. Much is left to oral explanation; examples from familiar experience and ordinary object-thinking had to be held to a minimum.

Were the content already known, the method of presentation would be a matter of simple pedagogical convenience. For this presentation, however, the case is more complex. It elaborates philosophy according to a method which, I hope, will be acknowledged as the only one that is identical with the development of its content.

To comprehend transitions from one philosophical sphere to another, to mediate them, is the Concept of philosophy. This methodical progression distinguishes philosophy from the external order in which other sciences may arrange their materials; it also distinguishes her from an arbitrary and fanciful mannerism often found in philosophical treatises.

This arbitrariness of form in philosophy corresponds to its merely subjective content. The necessity of comprehension is replaced by expressions of personal moods. Such adventures of thought may seem imposing for a while. Genuine and honest searchers for truth, however, will not be long deceived by mere pretensions of seriousness; behind them are lurking the dangers of whim and caprice —even insanity. Charlatans may hide from themselves the truth that their oracles are disguised trivialities; they nevertheless practice deception against themselves and the public.

At the opposite extreme, shallowness of thought produced a system of smart skepticism or smug criticalism. To have no part in comprehension is proudly proclaimed to be philosophy itself; the vanity and self-congratulation, implicit in this position, rose in proportion to the dearth of ideas.

Both directions of the spirit, romanticism and skepticism, have monkeyed quite a while with the earnestness of the German people. Its profound need for philosophy was misled and duped; the result was indifference to, even contempt of, scientific philosophy. Scoffing at philosophy became a favorite sport to those who in their self-conscious modesty do not in the least understand what is going on in the depth of comprehension—which even comprehends them.

Romanticism may partly be considered as the outcry of a youthful joy, greeting a new epoch, which has arisen in both the theoretical as well as the political realm. This joy saluted the dawn of a rejuvenated spirit with exuberance; however, it went immediately to enjoy the fruits of the Idea without laborious cultivation, and reveled in hopes and prospects which the new age promised. This rather reconciles us to its extravagances because there was a kernel of truth at the bottom, and because the superficial haze surrounding it was bound to evaporate and float away by itself.

Skepticism is more repulsive because it signifies weariness and impotence; it finds fault with the philosophical spirits of all centuries, and glosses them over with its own arrogance without recognizing its own sterility.

It is all the more enjoyable to perceive and to remark how, against both tendencies, the ultimate concern of higher cognition—the genuine love of wisdom—has maintained itself without self-conceit and vanity. This concern alone bestows on man his dignity. Sometimes this concern has expressed itself in the mode of immediate knowledge and feeling; to be interpreted as an impulsive testimony of an inherent far-reaching comprehensive insight. This interpretation would have to justify objective contents or values, contained in feeling as resulting from philosophical knowledge; and, even though the intuitionist seems to disdain the help philosophy could give him, he should nevertheless acknowledge his own dependence on it.

To the concern to *know* the truth I dedicate this attempt, offering it as an introduction or a contribution towards its fulfillment.

May such a purpose procure a favorable reception.

Heidelberg, May, 1817

FROM THE INAUGURAL ADDRESS
BERLIN, OCTOBER 22, 1818

(Hegel expresses his gratitude and his joy for having received the honor of becoming professor of philosophy at the University of Berlin; both *place* and historical *moment* are auspicious.)

The historical moment is auspicious: Peace in Europe after the Napoleonic wars may favor a rebirth of philosophy; this almost extinct Science may again raise its voice and may hope to receive attention and love.

The calamity of war-times exaggerates the importance of the most petty urgencies of daily worries; on the other hand, it draws all energies of the spirit into all-out efforts to save at least the framework of culture: To insure the survival of national existence and its political unity, the state. Such actual concerns were agitating all classes (Stände) of the people and were consuming all means and money; but also prevented that quietude or leisure in which the inner life of the spirit pursues its absolute concerns.

The world-spirit, engaged in actuality (Wirklichkeit) and violently torn asunder, was prevented to reflect on itself, to be at home with itself, and to gain proper familiarity with itself.

Now that this storm has blown over, the German nation has at least saved its independent nationality, which is the healthy soil of all living life; now the time has come when the free realm of thought may blossom forth in its freedom from the state—the political administration of the actual world.

The power and value of the spirit has been recognized in its own right: Only that is worth preserving and ought to be preserved which measures up to ideal standards; and can be justified by insight and thought.

And it is particularly this state which has ennobled itself by giving priority to the spirit; it has thereby gained an integrity and a cultural power which makes it equal to other states, even though they are its superiors in external power. Cultural power also has become a political actuality: The cultivation of science is an essential value in a sound political life; it is its very bloom.

Philosophy is the cultivation of truth; it is thereby essential to all sciences and cultural pursuits. It must be central to this central university, wherein philosophy must find its place and must be tended with utmost care . . . (Repetition: Casting off the yoke of foreign tyranny was the beginning of national freedom).

The ethical spirit made its power felt in actuality. We must honor and respect this power of feeling in which our generation has lived and acted; a feeling wherein moral, religious, and legal concerns were condensed, out of which the dignity of the spirit was actualized in a profound and all-embracing activity. The flatness and shallowness of daily interests and the corresponding superficiality of mere opinions were shown up in their nudity.

This deeper seriousness, having taken possession of the soul, is the true ground of philosophy; the needs of daily survival and the vanity of mere opinions are obstacles resisting it. If the soul is submerged and overtaken by them, no room is left to its comprehensive insight (Vernunft) which seeks no private gain for itself.

Our time is entrusted with the responsibility to

develop the substantial values of our religious, political, and scientific life.

A profound feeling for them is not enough, however it is only a promising seed. It must become a spiritual necessity to shake off lazy routines and to secure those substantial contents as our personal possession; this alone can rejuvenate our cultural life.

Moral and religious seriousness demand thorough and sterling qualities of work in all spheres of life. But to *know* them in their truth is the depth of the spirit giving account of itself for itself . . .

(The ordeal Germany has had to go through has made the Germans more philosophical than other nations.

This passage: Philosophy is abandoned by other nations and has sought refuge in Germany sounds nationalistic and ridiculous—as if philosophy were a displaced person asking for political asylum.

It is a typical example of Hegel's beloved mystifications; what seems immodest is in reality an excess of modesty or self-effacement. He is hiding behind—in this vase—a vague "Germany." Read in context and properly translated, this passage is a bit of disguised autobiography.

Hegel should have said something like this: Around 1800 I was desperate, anxious, and sorrowful (Wehmut, Sorge) about the helplessness and chaotic condition in Germany; this feeling prompted me to reflect on why Germany is not a state, and penned for myself a bitter and sarcastic critique of the so-called German Constitution. I still think that my feeling then was good and noble. It was one of the origins of my philosophizing. Since then, due mainly to the impact of the French Revolution and Napoleon, conditions have improved, but much is still to be done and we need philosophy as desperately as ever.)

To conserve the sacred light of philosophy has been entrusted to us; it is our calling to nurture and tend it; we must take care that the highest value of man, (note: not "German" man) self-comprehension of his essential nature, shall not be extinguished and lost (Repetition from the first Preface: The philosophical rebirth of Germany is threatened by blind adherence to tradition and authority; or by a scientism which asserts that only the knowledge of finite objects is real knowledge; or by replacing truth by subjective oracles or private hunches, or by a skeptical desperation for which the only truth is that no truth can be had).

One may even say: The prospect for philosophy in Germany has never been as bad as now; even though the currents of un-philosophy are reactionary shells of former conditions quite incompatible with the new substantial spirit.

I appeal to this new spirit and salute its dawn.

Withal, I appeal to the spirit of the young generation. It is a beautiful period of life when you are privileged to participate in the freedom of scientific endeavor without being hampered by material needs and distracted by momentary interests; and you are not yet corroded by skeptical smugness.

A sound heart still has the courage to demand truth; and the realm of truth is the home of philosophy at which she constantly works and which we share when we dedicate ourselves to her service.

What is true, great, and divine in life, is what it is by the virtue of the idea of truth. Philosophy aims to comprehend those essential values of life in their genuine shapes (Gestalt) and in their universal truth.

Nature realizes blindly what it must be; but in the realm of the spirit, freedom reigns. Whatever makes human life cohesive and coherent are values of the spirit; spirit is validated by itself and for itself; this realm of spiritual reality exists solely in the consciousness of truth and right, grasped as ideal totality (Ideen).

I may wish and hope that I shall succeed in winning and deserving your confidence as we start on our journey.

At first I can only beg you to trust in Science, to believe in comprehension, and to have confidence and faith in yourselves. The courage of truth—faith in the power of spirit—is the primal condition in the study of philosophy. Man ought to honor himself and deem himself worthy of the highest. He cannot think too much of the greatness and power of the spirit. The essence of the universe, closed though it is for itself, has no barrier to defend itself against the courage to know it. It must disclose its treasures; its depth is there for us to behold, to know, and to enjoy.

(These last sentences refer to the second and third part of Hegel's logic, entitled *Essence* and *Concept*. The essence of Being is that it is dialectical, but unknown to itself ("closed"). To know Being as dialectical is the conscious realization of it in the thinking person; Hegel calls this existing intelligibility Concept [Begriff].)

FROM THE *PREFACE* OF THE SECOND
EDITION OF THE *ENCYCLOPEDIA* (1827)

. . . knowledge of the truth is the one goal of my philosophical endeavors. The only road leading to truth is thought. It requires an unswerving will to truth, and courage—difficult to sustain—but it is the only way leading to permanent values for the spirit. Logical method alone can subdue thought leading to its own proper problem (Sache) and let it dwell therein. This problem is the Absolute; at first thought must ask special questions which seem to be deviations or detours, but it is through such detours that the Absolute is restored in the end and in the freest medium of the spirit.

(Examples of such deviations: Sciences and education, rational enlightenment and religious concerns, natural laws and positive laws, national culture and the political state.)

These opposites, which for a while seemed to coexist peacefully, became antagonistic. Their divorce and clash made philosophy necessary: The spirit reconciles itself with itself in comprehending and embracing its own opposites, without glossing over their differences.

It is the worst prejudice to set off philosophy as if it were something special by itself, apart from those concrete shapes (Gestalten) of life. Meaningful scientific experience or the comprehensive actuality of right; pure, unbiased religion and simple loyalty must be acknowledged and justified in and by philosophy; philosophical reflection learns from them and is nourished and fortified by them.

This genuine objective content, *evident in great intuitions of nature, history, and art, and reflected in thought, is the speculative Idea itself.*

(Hegel then repeats the criticism of the first *Preface* against rationalism and scientism; and against the romantic irrationalism and skeptical subjectivism.

He also repeats that philosophical truth may reside in religious imagination: "Religion can exist without philosophy, but philosophy cannot be itself without including religion"; truth also may reside in nonreligious intuitive thinkers. Jakob Böhme, Heinrich Jacobi, and Franz von Bader are mentioned as representatives of philosophical feeling and content without logical form and method.

New in the second preface is the following defence of this philosophy against malicious interpretations.)

Reason has rightly noticed that speculative thought is not merely rational; but has no inkling that its own formal categories of object-thinking are comprehended in comprehension (Vernunft), but are not sufficient to comprehend it. It does not even occur to the rationalist that he would have to undergo a conversion before touching philosophy. Instead of that, the rationalist naïvely goes on to apply his own abstract principle of identity to a concrete spiritual unity and nicknames it: "Identify-system." He does not understand that in ridiculing it, he is ridiculing his own rationalistic and lifeless misconception of unity. He claims that everything in this system is declared to be the same: As if good and evil, subject and object, finite and infinite, etc., were the same.

In a concrete spiritual unity such polarities indeed do not simply fall apart (like rotten fish) but are self-distinctions within it, and are also preserved in their difference.

But to formal reason, truth remains forever a mystery. Truth has rightly been said to be the standard of itself and its own opposite, the false; it is "index sui et falsi." What is known as false is known in its truth; but falseness cannot know truth.

The philosophical Concept (Begriff) understands itself, but also understands those shapes of life which do not understand themselves, even though they may possess a kernel of truth; if they do understand their own truth, they already are in philosophy.

Philosophy understands feeling and faith; but it cannot be judged from standpoints which have placed themselves outside of philosophical self-criticism. To judge philosophy one must participate in it as it progresses and unfolds itself.

I welcome such critical cooperation, which alone I can consider and respect.

Berlin, May 25, 1827.

THE ENCYCLOPEDIA

OF PHILOSOPHICAL SCIENCES

DIALECTIC AND THE FACTUAL SCIENCES.

(Hegel's own title: "Preliminary Note on Theories of Knowledge," is misleading: There is no "preliminary note," but his *crucial definition of dialectic;** and there is not a word about "theories of knowledge," but a clear-cut contra-distinction of dialectic and the non-dialectical methods and materials of factual sciences.)

§1

All the sciences, except philosophy, deal with objects which are taken for granted. Items of investigation are accepted as given prior to scientific inquiry; in turn, interpretations proferred in the process of investigation, are verified again by reference to objective data. Sciences do not need to justify the ontological status of their objects. Mathematics, jurisprudence, medicine, zoology, botany, and so on, quite legitimately assume such things as magnitude, space, number, right, sickness, animals, plants, and so on.

As an initial step, the objects of study are named. These verbal stipulations fix the objects. Thereupon, further determinations, still derived from immediate observation, are added. Here, however, a difficulty comes into focus: On the one hand these determina-

---

* According to the Hegel legend he has merely *practiced* dialectic, but never said what dialectic *is;* see also §13 ff.

tions are supposed to be features of the object investigated; on the other hand they are essences in thought; formal-logical definitions and classifications. This dual claim gives rise to much controversy. To question as to the *necessity* and *reality* of such claims and such objects is not the concern of the several sciences.

§2

The case with philosophy is different. Philosophy begins in controversy and doubt; it begins with a question about itself.

Its object cannot be coped with in object-thinking; it not only cannot be given in an object-image (Vorstellung); it is even opposed to factual representation. The latter must be lifted above itself and brought to know itself in its limitation; this would be its philosophical *critique*.

§3

The object and method of philosophy are not known beforehand; their deployment is philosophy itself. This is the perplexity of its form: On the one hand, philosophy must immediately begin with itself; on the other hand, it is a mediation of all things. This necessary unity of immediacy and mediation is the *Concept* (Begriff) of philosophy.

One could, if one wanted to, show that a vague notion of philosophy is implicit in ordinary thinking. One might begin with immediate sensuous perception and appetite, and show that man is soon driven beyond immediacy towards a feeling and presentiment of something higher than himself—an infinite being and infinite will. I have followed this course in my *Phenomenology of Mind*.

Or one might resort to such appealing questions as: What is the soul, what is the world, what is

God? What can I know, how shall I act, what may I hope?

Also religion may be a starting point, beginning in feeling, but also offering instructions and solutions. None of these alternatives, however, are beyond doubt and negation.

Doubt and critique is the unique method whereby contents become philosophically appropriated—unless investigated, they remain popular notions.

Many imagine that they are philosophical when they find reality in this immediate feeling or accept it on hearsay, but such immediacy of experience is not comprehension (Vernunft). The truth of philosophy can be derived only from its object, *reality*, and from its own necessary Concept, and not from authority or from a general consensus of opinions.

One readily sees what happens to philosophy when it is supposed to be derived from external experience. Newton and the British empiricists confuse experimental physics with philosophy; they call electrical and magnetic appliances, pumps and the like, philosophical instruments. They have a journal, entitled "Annals of Philosophy or Magazine of Chemistry, Minerology, Mechanics, Natural History, Agriculture, and the Arts." They mistake impressions and opinions *about* the given for philosophy.

§4

My remark that philosophy can be developed only out of its own generating problem is a mere anticipation, which is as deniable as it is undeniable; it is intended to introduce philosophy to the reader in the manner of an historical tale.

§5

Philosophy is the *Science* (Wissenschaft) of *Comprehensiveness* (Vernunft) wherein the totality of Being becomes aware of itself; Being is identical with its own comprehensiveness.

All other sciences are concerned with the knowledge of finite things; they are finite kinds of knowledge. Reason (Verstand) is their principle; it is the correlation of finite subjects and given objects. Reason functions without self-knowledge. Even when objects, such as laws, duties, and values exist in consciousness for reason, they are still particular objects over against the consciousness which is aware of them.

Religion is closer to philosophy than the sciences of reason. Its object is an infinite Being which is supposed to father and to govern all other beings. The difficulty lies in such personalized image-language. Religious images fall apart. (The "good shepherd" is also "the wrath of the lamb.") The creature and the Creator are pictured as if they were two persons. The highest *truth* of religion is nevertheless also an unfathomable, unknowable *secret*. The religious image is a Given which is to remain external to the very religious consciousness which produces this distinction. Truth is present in religion, but it is present in all sorts of feelings, representations (Vorstellung), presentiments; in motley processes of worship, thoughtful sometimes—but still truth not in the form of truth. The religious soul is all-embracing; nevertheless it carves out for itself a particular region which is kept apart from the other functions of consciousness.

Philosophy may also be considered the Science of freedom; the foreignness of objects in correlation with the finitude of consciousness is comprehended in freedom (aufgehoben, aufheben: To cancel, to preserve, to elevate); longing, dependence, and anxiety are overcome. Only in philosophy is comprehension (Vernunft) at home with itself, comprehending also contingencies, natural pressures, and all sorts of relations to externality within itself. Philosophy liberates man from them and elevates him above them, without denying their irrational reality.

Science of comprehensiveness is neither one-sided or merely rational—nor a private property or a peculiar talent. Likewise it is not a heavenly favor —or disfavor—and certainly not the oracle of artistic genius (against Schelling). Since it is nothing but comprehensiveness in itself as well as for itself, it is essentially that which we share and in which we share.

It is not an idealism in which the content of knowledge is through and through subjective, imprisoning its products within the subject; subject and object are only distinct, but necessary, poles within comprehensive, universal concreteness. The contrast of idealistic and realistic philosophy is of no importance; such expressions as subjectivity and objectivity, reality and ideality, are simply bare abstractions.

(Historians have labelled Hegel's philosophy "absolute idealism"—this is just as pointless as any other "ism," even though the "Idea" is a central term, equivalent to and exchangeable with "reality as such," "world-itself," "universe," "Comprehensiveness," the "Absolute." See §161. His "absolute idealism" might just as well be called "absolute realism," but is neither, because any standpoint which has an opposite is not the Absolute.)

All Being is *Comprehensiveness conscious of itself.*

§6

Philosophy is the *Encyclopedia of philosophical Sciences.* Its self-engendered movement is free, but each of its steps is necessary; it distinguishes its disciplines or "parts" and links them all together. Each of its "parts" is itself a philosophical whole. Each encompasses in itself a self-completing sphere in which the whole is present. The Oneness of this whole is nevertheless determined differently in its many particularized elements or media. The presence of the whole in each of its singular spheres renders each a whole; each contains this insufficiency and this longing to break its own restricting barrier and to en-whole itself. Each sphere is established in itself as well as grounded in and by a negative relation to further spheres. The whole becomes systematically articulate, therefore, as a *circle of circles of which each is a necessary moment of the whole movement.*

§7

Philosophy is *essentially* encyclopedic, that is, encompassing or encircling. In distinguishing as well as connecting its own self-distinctions, the whole is both the necessity of its parts as well as its own freedom. The *Truth* can only exist as such a totality systematically developed; only the whole is the truth.

Unsystematic philosophizing is not Scientific or dialectical. It may express an inner orientation or a private worldview. It is accidental and contingent in its contents. If it is not justified as moment of the whole and resting on unexamined premises or presuppositions, it possesses only a private inner *certainty.* Truth moves forward through critically comprehended certainties.

§8

It is a mistake to confuse systematic philosophy with a system that is deduced or derived from a single principle. (Hegel's usual trick! He takes a term—here "system"—robs it of all common and customary dictionary-meaning ("falsely so called") and then calmly proceeds to use it in his own stubborn way as no one else ever uses it—and then complains that no one can understand him.

So, when he says here, "philosophy is system," he wants us to understand that philosophy is anything but a system!

The same holds for "science," "concept," and many other key terms. It makes perfectly good sense, however, to say that systematic philosophy is not a closed system, or that it is an "open system.")

To pit one system against another is to pit philosophy against herself. True philosophy comprehends all such one-sided principles in itself. Systematic philosophy, as well as the history of philosophy, shows this; the various philosophies which appear in history are, on the one hand, the One philosophy on different levels of its maturity, and on the other hand the particular principles of particular systems. Both are branches of one and the same whole.

This oneness and wholeness of systematic philosophy in partial or particular systems implies the proper dialectical-logical relation of *universal* and *particular*. Formal logic defines the universal as an abstract generality outside its particulars; as abstracted and isolated, it becomes another particular. Even in common life the universal, in isolation, would strike one as inadequate and odd; as if one who has demanded fruit would refuse cherries, pears, grapes, etc., because they were cherries, pears, or grapes, but not fruit. With reference to philosophy, however, one justifies its disdainful rejection with the excuse that there are so many philosophies, each having *one* philosophy but not *the* philosophy—as if cherries were not also fruit!

Or one extols a system with a general principle over others with only partial principles; or one even puts philosophy on a par with doctrines which assert that there is no such thing as philosophy; or one uses its name for a scientism which presupposes that truth can be found exclusively in that which is immediately given, serving as an occasion for further reflections about it.

The task of an encyclopedic presentation of philosophy is to state the origins and basic concepts of philosophical disciplines. To accomplish this task, the peculiar problems of every sphere must be clarified in detail and in context.

If a philosophical discipline belongs to truth, it must be a totality—not an isolated piece of information. Out of context it would be undirected and wholly random; as such it could not constitute a complete discipline or Science. As *context* of its disciplines, the whole of philosophy is One Science.

§10

Any one of the disciplines is true by virtue of its inclusion in that philosophy which comprehends all the disciplines. Thus the philosophical encyclopedia is distinguished from the ordinary one. The latter, at best, is an aggregate of sciences, taken up in an accidental and empirical fashion. Among them are even many which are sciences in name only; actually they are merely collections of informations, alphabetically arranged. Such encyclopedias must always fail to show any necessary connection, and their information remains provisional and must always be brought up to date. In sharp contrast, the philosophical encyclopedia must exclude mere aggregates of information.

A threefold distinction will clarify the meaning of philosophy as Science in relation to the other sciences.

Sciences, such as philology and heraldry, simply furnish aggregates of informations. The basis of their knowledge is arbitrary, irrational, positive.

(Hegel's perverse use of the term "positive" goes back to his earliest writing. For example in his "Positivity of the Christian Religion" he describes everything that is irrational, superstitious, tyrannical, authoritarian, and negative in it by the term positive.")

Other sciences are also "positive"; yet at the same time they proceed from a rational principle. As "positive" they are distinguished from others by their material and are named accordingly; as rational they share in philosophy. All sciences which pursue their own course within a universal philosophical sphere, even if they seem to disregard philosophy, belong to this group. They seek to introduce general truth into the empirical world of singular and irrational events. Their intention or end is to establish causal relations in areas of contingencies. In this, their struggle, they are manifestations of the dialectical Concept, although they are not aware of this.

In the science of law, for example, the system of direct and indirect taxes requires detailed and exact prescriptions. Wide possibilities are left open which may be decided upon by causal determinations of the greatest variety. Uncertainties and quarrels about them never end. Such decisions are external to, but comprehended in, the *Concept of Right*, which is a complete reality existing in itself as well as for itself.

The Idea of *Nature*, likewise, appears in endless singular contingencies. Natural history, descriptions of the earth, and medical science determines natural objects by subordinated and coordinated classifications; they depend on the irrationality of that which happens or chances to appear.

History is in a similar situation. On the one hand it is an essential *Idea*, and on the other hand its appearances are spreading out in a field of contingency and irrationality.

Such sciences become "positive" in the dogmatic sense of the word, when they do not know that their concepts are finite only. They then take them for granted as if they were ultimately real and valid. They fail to understand that their whole sphere is limited and is in need of transition to a higher one.

Their theory of knowledge is the theory of finitude, expressing the dualism of given content and of abstract logical form. It is partly rationalistic, partly irrationalistic (begrifflos). This leaves feeling, faith, authority, all inner and outer intuition of value, without cognitive justification. Religion, as well as philosophy, is supposed to be founded in nothing save anthropological or physiological facts of consciousness.

Sometimes it happens that only the epistemological theory of the sciences is rationalistic or irrationalistic in the sense of a radical empiricism. In the sciences themselves, the inner consistency of the Concept may nevertheless shine through; it unites meaningful intentions and logical organizations of appearance. A unity of manifold opposites in a concrete process may then be evident in spite of the external, irrational, accidental nature of that which is apprehended. A meaningful experimental physics or history would thus mirror the comprehensiveness of nature and of human deeds and records.

§11

In distinction from all other sciences, philosophy envisages the problem of *reality as such*. The whole of philosophical knowledge is the presentation of this Idea; it articulates and understands itself. The Idea is comprehensiveness realizing itself and reality comprehending itself. To become for itself, what it is in itself, reality must oppose itself to itself; yet it must remain one and the same in this, its own otherness.

Boiled down to a formula: Philosophy is divided into three parts. *Logic* is the cognition of the Idea as it is in and for itself; philosophy of *Nature* is the cognition of the same Idea in its own otherness; philosophy of the *Spirit* (Geist) is the cognition of the Idea as it returns to itself from its otherness.

This division should be understood as a mere

76

pedagogical device, and formula for memory and reason. The distinctions of the Concept of philosophical cognition can be realized only by going through the whole process of self-knowledge. Cognition is this process. The formula merely anticipates that which can be actualized in its necessity only if the Idea itself is proceding thus, in its own self-differentiation. As mentioned above, the essential philosophical disciplines are all self-determination of the Idea which remains the same in all its different media. The same Idea of the whole is recognized in nature as well as in mind: In nature it is recognized in the form of self-alienation; in mind it is recognized as becoming for itself what it is in itself.

Every determination in which the idea appears is a fluid moment in the self-realization of freedom. Every essential aspect of the world viewed is an objective being evident to the worldview which is its organ.

Philosophy has no static parts dealing with general kinds of substances outside of one another. If our division of philosophy is misunderstood in this manner—as external object-image (Vorstellung)—it would be misleading indeed.

Each discipline is living whole in the comprehensive living whole.

THE LOGIC OF PHILOSOPHY

SYSTEMATIC INTRODUCTION

§12

Logic as logic of philosophy develops the Idea of the whole of reality in the abstract medium of thought: This definition of logic, in turn, is the result of logic itself. A prime example of the fact that the determinations of logic grow out of and are grounded in a whole, which is present in its entirety to the logician.

Usually, logic is said to be the science of thought —its determinations and laws. But to say this implies self-knowledge, an identity of knowledge with itself. Thus it is that dialectic is the all-pervasive method manifest in each function of Logic—even in formal logic. The Idea determines itself in a totality of functions in which it produces itself.

Logic, thus conceived, is both difficult and simple. Geometry can appeal to abstract intuitions, commonsense to sensuous perceptions; logic does not have this advantage. It requires at once the power to concentrate on thoughts as such—bracketing out experiential contents—and to integrate manifold thoughts into a whole and living movement.

On the other hand, logic is the easiest of the sciences. Its contents are determinations of the same thinking which reflects on them: They are as simple as they are familiar.

Logic has a utility value. It produces a cultivated mind. Man matures in his practice of thought, and in his reflection upon it. Utility, however, is not the highest value of logic. The term "logical" is equivalent to "truthful"; logic is truth in the form of truth.

§13

There are three aspects in every thought which is logically real or true: The abstract or rational form, which says what something is; the dialectical negation, which says what something is not; the speculative—concrete comprehension: A is also that which it is not, A is non-A. These three aspects do not constitute three parts of logic, but are moments of everything that is logically real or true. They belong to every philosophical Concept. Every Concept is rational, is abstractly opposed to another, and is united in comprehension together with its opposites. *This is the definition of dialectic.*

§14

Thinking as *reason* (Verstand) requires fixed or identical determinations in clear distinction from other identities. To reason, such limited abstractions are evident as valid and as real.

§15

The dialectical movement, in contrast to reason, cancels such one-sided determinations. Dialectically they are related to that which they are not. It is this negative relation which defines them. They themselves require their opposites, and are determined by them. When dialectic is exclusively rational, it leads to *skepticism*. Reason, as isolated aspect of dialectic, points to the untruth of every thought.

Historically, dialectic is considered a sophistic trick which arbitrarily and deliberately produces confusion in conception. This confusion, it is supposed, is destroyed by reason; and this formal destruction of illusions is proudly proclaimed as truth. Reason as the correction of all one-sided determinations and of historical misconceptions remains tied to their irrationality. In comprehending reason as such a struggle, dialectical reflection passes beyond or transcends reason.

While rational terms are preserved in their limited validity, they belong to complex relationships in which they constantly change their functions. Dialectic is not an external reflection, but belongs immanently to the transitoriness of all finite, one-sided, and merely rational positions. It is their own negation which they are, without knowing it. It is the moving soul of the world-as-process. It guarantees to philosophy the immanent connection or necessary consistency between its contrary and essential disciplines.

§16

Speculative comprehension grasps and is the unity of all essential opposites. It is the principle of systematic philosophizing. In realizing the limitation of every finite standpoint, it realizes the infinity of Being through the non-finality in all finite beings. The Absolute maintains itself in the transition of all its own non-absolute or partial manifestations.

The positive result of dialectic is not an abstract void, an abyss into which everything is thrown. Dialectic denies absolutely one thing alone: The claim that any particular thing of the finite world exists absolutely. The Absolute appears as *"nothing"* to those finite positions which want to cling to their pseudo-absolute claims. This does not mean that "nothing is." To suppose this is to confuse thoughtlessly the dialectical-ontological negation with a formal-logical self-contradiction, wherein reason isolates the negative function of comprehensiveness as if it were a simple identity beyond all definite contents. Rather, the identity of speculative comprehension is the concrete unity of all essential opposites in the world itself. This alone is the ultimate concern of philosophy. The abstractions of reason are pierced, so that reason may reach its own concrete thought.

The logic of philosophy retains and includes the formal logic of reason. Leave out dialectical comprehension and formal logic remains! Formal logic may unravel the tale of finite object-thinking in the sciences; if the story of the sciences is absolutized, science degenerates into scientism.

§17

Concepts of philosophy are concrete realities and values of Being, thought together with their opposites. Philosophy contemplates them as they are in themselves as well as what they are for those to which they are evident. Contents are thereby realized as manifestation of Being, which is both in and for itself; or which relates itself to itself in an eternal movement. The ontological categories are thus also the foundation for the self-comprehension of mind and spirit. Form and content of Concepts are not abstractly separated. As self-manifestations and self-determinations of the living whole, they are at once its forms as well as its value-contents.

The formal logic of reason, on the other hand, handles forms in abstraction from contents. Neither form nor content expresses self-knowledge. Since they are not true for themselves, they are not forms of living truth. It is even essential that material data of formal logic remain alien to their forms. The logic of speculative philosophy, in contrast, thinks that which is real in and for itself. The Absolute is present in the subject thinking it. The Concept is absolute in thinking subjects together in their unity, as well as

84

in their difference. Concept (noesis noeseos) is what Aristotle called the principle of his First Philosophy or metaphysics.

As Concept (Begriff), reality becomes conscious of itself in the thinking mind. Herein philosophy seems to be occupied exclusively with the thinking mind and sundered from the richness of the sensuous world; and from the more concrete and intelligible historical world. But the dialectic of philosophy is not confined to the actual subject: It pertains equally to the structures of Being, to essential universals. Philosophy, in this enlarged sense, is cognition of reality as such.

The dialectic of philosophy also is present in the oppositeness of essential universal structures of Being (ontology); also the realistic treasures of the world presuppose onto-logic. These treasures also belong to the all-pervasive ultimacy of Truth. The concrete universals abstractly presented in logic prefigure all essential values of the spirit. The highest among them is religion.

On its highest plane philosophy contemplates the Concept of all Concepts, the eternal Absolute—the God who is worshipped in religion. Philosophy then culminates in speculative theology.

Historical Introduction

§18

Logic as the logic of speculative philosophy re-places what used to be called metaphysics. It evolved through the history and critique of meta-physics, maturing, as it were, in purgatory. Matured, logic is Science. Because of the development in the advent of logic, we must acquaint ourselves with the problems of metaphysics and understand how their logical truths burst through their historical shells. Metaphysics is not a pastime for mere anti-quarian curiosity. It was engrossed in persistent problems, which are the very problems of logic. Its main defect was that it approached them from a rationalistic point of view (Verstandes-Ansicht).

§19

Rationalism erred in identifying categories of thought with the principles of given things. Its assumption, Being can be truly thought or makes itself available in thought, is a high principle—higher than the negative or skeptical scientism of recent vintage. But it failed when the Absolute was thought as if it were a thing consisting of general rational predicates. Rationalism did not evaluate critically the categories of Reason (Verstandes-Bestimmungen); let alone their competence to determine the Absolute. External object—science and metaphysics were tangled up in a knot. For example, existence (Dasein) is not a formal-logical predicate as it is used in the proposition "God has existence." Finite and infinite, simple and complex, one and many, are dialectical opposites: They must be viewed together. Therefore the questions of reason: Is the world finite *or* infinite? Is the soul simple *or* complex? Is the thing a one *or* a whole? are meaningless.

§20

The problems of metaphysics were comprehensive totalities, such as the *soul*, the *world*, *God*—but rationalism treated them as if they were object-images (Vorstellung) of given finished things. It applied categories of reason to them as object-sciences do to things, and in doing so demonstrated that object-thinking cannot furnish a sufficient standard of absolute problems.

Assuming that the formal-logical laws of contradiction and of the excluded middle were laws of Reality, metaphysics became *dogmatic*. Seeing that contradictory contentions cannot both be true—if the one is true, the other must be false—metaphysics failed to see that this law is valid only for finite situations. In no sense is it relevant when applied to absolute totalities (examples in §20).

§22

Ontology is one of the major parts of metaphysics: the study of the essence of Being. For *rationalism* the essence of Being is studied in abstraction from the manifold particulars of finite existence. The contents of the finite world were blindly accepted as empirical and contingent only. Thus rationalism lost itself in empty forms of reason. *Empiricism*, in turn, fell greedily on data; its goal was to get as many particulars together as possible. For *Nominalism* knowledge became nothing but a formally consistent use of language and correct definition of terms. Correct analysis was unconcerned with truth and its necessity. Universals are mere labels to be placed on particulars. In all these ventures, the lack of a dialectical principle, uniting the finite and the essence of Being, left the reality-value of both undetermined.

The formal-logical rule of consistency holds for ordinary propositions. The predicate must not be predicated of the subject of the proposition if this implies self-contradiction. But propositions of object-thinking are not ontological. The ontological Concept is a concrete unity of opposite distinctions. Truth, therefore, is not merely the absence of formal-logical contradictions. The necessary correlation of essential being and finite existence, of simplicity and com-

87

plexity, etc., constitutes the dialectical Concept. Such ontological terms become contradictory only in formal-logical sentences. In their necessary correlation and in correlation with thought thinking them, they exemplify Being which is true both in and for itself.

§23

The second part of metaphysics was called *rational psychology*. Its fallacy consisted in treating the soul or spirit as a given thing or object—without reflection that the soul meets itself in its self-estrangement.

The problem of immortality was mixed up with temporal changes, quantitative compositions, and qualitative degrees. They have their legitimate place in a sphere where increases and decreases can be measured.

§24

The third part of metaphysics, *cosmology*, dealt with the world. Its over-all problems are: Eternity and spatial-temporal finitude; necessity and contingency; formal laws and irrational changes; freedom of man and the origin of evil; efficient and final cause or purpose; essence and appearance, substance and existence; form and matter; happiness and misery; good and evil.

In dealing with these dialectical relations, the opposites were either over-emphasized or falsely absolutized.

§25

The fourth part of metaphysics, *natural* or *rational theology*, contemplated the concept of God or the possibility thereof. In so doing, it developed proofs of his existence and theories of his attributes.

Rationalism erred in misunderstanding the speculative Concept. It either objectified the Absolute as if it were a person over against the subject; or emptied the Absolute so that it became a vague being-in-general or essence, devoid of all concrete determinations.

An absolute *dualism* is posited between the world, which is declared to be nothing or something positively evil; and God, who is to be considered to be all that the world is not, and absolutely good. This cleavage leaves nothing to be desired for either side. While the contradiction is perfect, it simply says the same thing twice. Thus the failure of all rational theology is clear: It is unable to see that a dialectical negation is also an affirmative relation. If infinity is thought by itself, apart from the finitude of the existing world, then infinity itself becomes something finite; it is limited by this otherness of the world.

A further error of rational theology lies in the perverse assumption that the existence of God depends upon, or is mediated by reasons—as if he were a conclusion in a syllogism (Verstandes-Identität der Bestimmtheiten).

The circular reasoning of *idealism* is no better. For it the name God simply describes a state of a subjective pious consciousness. It then asks how all other concepts of God agree with its own subjectivistic preconception.

A truly religious emancipation from the finite world cannot be achieved if the transition from the finite to the infinite is not an interacting process of both. As long as reason insists on splitting the Absolute into separate objects over against each other, it can never escape its own contradictions. The attributes of God are, on the one hand, exaggerations of moral values such as justice, kindness, power, wisdom; but on the other hand, they all denied him because none of them is infinite. They sink to the level of an edifying nebulous chatter.

§26

Rationalistic metaphysics succumbed to attacks which came from two opposite directions. The first was led by *empiricism*. It took its stand in immediate experience, which was either sensuous and external or psychic and internal. The empiricist believed he was able to derive all contents of thought from given facts of consciousness; at the same time, in contradistinction to this, he believed that formal-logical analysis of empirical facts—formal abstraction and identities—is the source of truth. The supersensuous Absolute was either radically denied or agnostically doubted.

§27

Kant criticized both rationalistic and empiristic metaphysics. He questioned the validity of reason for metaphysics. Its categories, he asserted, were synthetic propositions a priori of rational form and non-rational content, valid only for scientific experience or object-thinking; they are not derivable from the senses, but from the spontaneity of thought, creating universal, necessary, objective relations.

§28

The transcendental unity of self-consciousness— I am identical in all my thinking—is the original derivation and justification of all categories; they all unify experience.

The manifold object-images, given to feeling and perception, are the empirical contents which are located by the forms of sensibility, space and time; they are thereby outside of one another. These contents are then thought by logical forms. Contents and forms are opposite in an original identity. Such is

Kant's apperception of consciousness: I think and connect objects and also relate them to myself; the categories of reason are ways by which I unify the object in myself. (As Kant puts it: The conditions which make true judgments possible are the same conditions which make the objects of judgment real.)

§29

While immediate perception is elevated to the rank of scientific experience by the objectivity of rational categories, their use is nevertheless restricted to experience. Without the given materials they are empty.

§30

On account of this finitude of reason, scientific object-knowledge is incapable of determining the Absolute, because it is given in no perception.

§31

Insight into the limited character or conditional nature of object-sciences rests on our ability to think the unconditional whole. In its light the scientific objects are known as appearance. This is comprehension (Vernunft).

Kant, however, underrates the impact of his own notion of comprehension. He refers to the Infinite as if it were a thing; and suggest that if reason is to know this thing-in-itself, as it knows other things, it produces necessary self-contradictions, antinomies. If it is to know the soul in the same manner as if it were a given object, the necessary self-contradictions involved is the fallacy of paralogism. Comprehension is thus reduced to reason (Verstand); and reason, which ought to unify experience, is unable to fulfill this demand. The difficulty is again clear: Reason can be critical only of object-metaphysics; it cannot be an organ of truth.

§32

In its critique of the finitude of the categories of reason, critical philosophy is right. But it is one-sided in that it fails to comprehend its own comprehensiveness. The dialectical tension between logical, organizing form and organized, irrational material is not understood as a concrete logical process. Kant does not realize that he is not practicing rational scientific logic when he comprehends it in its limited truth.

A further deficiency in Kant is his lack of a systematic-dialectical determination of the categories. He depends on empiricism and formal logic. If this were remedied, the transcendental unity of self-consciousness would cease to be a mere formal unity. There are many syntheses a priori or concrete unities of opposites in which the unity of self-consciousness manifests and determines itself; and its categories—the categories of comprehensions, including those of scientific reason—determine each other mutually and in the whole; each is that which it is, by being also that which it is not. This mutual dialectical relation justifies them systematically (deduziert).

Kant's mannerism and love of formalistic schemes must not let us overlook his merits. He has accomplished the profoundest and most decisive progress in the philosophy of recent times. He demonstrated that dialectical opposites are necessary and essential in and for the comprehensive whole. Reason makes them articulate, but it should not confuse its formal-logical contradictions with the ontological reality of the opposites. Equally important is Kant's emphasis of the ontological status and reality of the soul. He has rescued this problem from object-metaphysics and from an empiristic meaningless question. The genuine and essential reality of the soul lies in its identity with its own self-experience; the "I am" is a being which knows and is the self-knowledge which exists. In grasping this appearance of *freedom* as the essence as well as the existence of the soul, the absolute first ground of philosophy has been reached.

§33

These objective values, however, are obscured by Kant's standpoint, which is subjective *idealism* or *criticalism*. It disagrees with empiricism as to what constitutes experience; but agrees with it that there can be no comprehension of the all-comprehensive Absolute, because knowledge is said to be restricted to sensuous stuff. It remains tied to the finite which is never ultimately real, and to an object-knowledge which wavers between the poles of subjectivity and externality.

§34

Further, Kant's criticism contradicts his own concept of knowledge. On the one hand, scientific reason alone furnishes objective knowledge, but on the other hand, it only furnishes knowledge of appearance to finite observers. In this self-limitation of objective reason, the comprehensive Idea or the Concept of absolute truth is lost when Comprehension is degraded to a regulative formal unity; and the absolute Being to an empty thing-in-itself.

It is of the uttermost inconsistency to admit that reason is confined to know appearances only, and at the same time to contend that this is the only true knowledge we have. A deficient, incomplete, limited mode of knowledge can only be known in comparison with the really-present Idea of a complete whole. It is sheer unconsciousness not to realize that by this dialectical negation of one side, which thereby is known to be finite and limited, a true knowledge is practiced. It proves the reality and the presence of an unlimited Infinite.

Also religious and moral life presuppose knowledge of the Absolute to be true; it is implied in them. Both have overcome the abstract separation of being in itself from being for itself. The Absolute is not merely a negative Beyond but it comprehends and dissolves the negativity of finite, fixed and subjective standpoints within itself.

This agreement between dialectical ontology and the practical spirit in ethics and religion also eliminates Kant's division of theoretical and practical reason. Likewise the atomistic division of the soul contradicts the complete unity of self-consciousness. The faculties of the soul do not dwell in separate compartments. What would practical reason be, if it were not a synthesis a priori, or manifestation of dialectical truth?

§35

When philosophy reaches logical maturity, it is *Science*. It requires abandoning all dogmatic assumptions, subjective presupposition, and one-sided standpoints.

We have illustrated this self-criticism of philosophy in four standpoints; First, *rationalism* assumes the fixed validity of concepts of reason, even though they oppose and modify one another; second, *objectivism* assumes finished and given objects to function as a standard of thought, but when the two sides are compared the question of inadequate cognition cannot be answered; third, *formalism* treats knowledge as a relation of formally defined terms, and is *skepticism* in regard to an indefinite substratum; fourth, *dualism* assumes a subject of knowledge over against

94

an object of knowledge. Both are independent of each other and both *shall* but never *can* meet.

§36

Philosophy as *Science* contains all such assumptions with itself but also shows why it cannot rest satisfied with any one of them. Every assumption is criticized by thinking through the consequences of its own contention. Seen as false in its exclusiveness, it is abandoned; seen as the criticism implicit in its own standpoint, it is transcended. The Logic of philosophy or philosophy as Science assumes nothing but itself as the critical movement of thought.

This self-critical movement appears in historical life. One-sided assumptions occurring in Logic as moments of pure thought are also found in immediate consciousness; it is engaged in belaboring a given world. Its object-images, representations, opinions, and presuppositions are the given problems of and for philosophical critique; it shows why they must be given up or why they are given as problems (Das Gegebene ist aufgegeben).

I have previously told this story in my *Phenomenology of Mind.* It was intended to be a first part or introduction to philosophy leading up to the logic or Science of philosophy and terminating in its Concept.

But further, the critical history of consciousness is also an organic member in the infinite circle of philosophy. Like every other philosophical discipline, it is not *the* beginning, but *a* beginning. The absolute beginning is the whole movement of comprehension.

This movement might also be presented as a total *skepticism* in which all finite forms of cognition meet their doom. But in its abstract isolation, this negative dialectic is just as unsatisfactory as any other abstract standpoint. It is, as mentioned before, an essential function within the speculative logic of philosophy. The decision to think radically, to call everything into question, to make everything problematic, and to be trapped by nothing, is both a complete doubt and desperation (Zweifel und Verzweiflung) as well as a complete freedom which grasps in the breakdown of all uncertainties, in the uncertainty of all things finite, the infinite certainty of itself which is one and the same as thought pure and simple.

The Logic of philosophy must fulfill Kant's demand of a total comprehension comprehending itself through the critique of all its essential manifestations of faculties.

§37

Pure Science or Logic is divided into four branches (see editor's note §139). Logic of Being qua Being or ontology; Logic of Essence, in which Being is understood to be essentially dialectical; Logic of the Concept, in which the dialectical nature of Being becomes intelligible for itself; Logic of the Idea, in which all opposites are actualized in a teleological process. All opposites in reality are also opposites in philosophical reflection. Reality is in thought, thought is in reality.

Logic includes *thought in so far as it is just as much world-itself as it is thought,* or *world-itself in so far as it is just as much concrete, universal thought.* World-conceptions unfold themselves in self-consciousness or in the form of self: This subject-object world-contents make it impossible for a logic of phi- which exists and is intelligible in and for itself; and in the Idea, which is teleological movement or final cause, in which the Concept is a moment. These world-contents make it impossible for a logic of philosophy to be merely formal; if we wish still to employ the word *matter,* then the genuine matter of philosophy is at the same time formal self-differentiations of the Absolute. Logic is the realm of pure comprehension and truth as it is in and for itself. . . .*

I could not, of course, imagine that the method I have followed would not be open to much improvement and elaboration; at the same time I know it is the only method which is not separable from its objective content: Dialectic is not an external reflection, but the movement of the content in itself. Thus it is that philosophical expositions may be regarded as Scientific only as they conform to the course and rhythm of world-itself.

In accord with this method I would observe further that the divisions and headings, sections, and chapters of the book, which are given in their work are made for the purposes of a preliminary survey; they have, in fact, only *historical* value. They do not belong to the content and body of the Science, but are compiled by external reflection, which, having already run through the whole of the scheme, knows and indicates the sequence in advance of its actual presentation. (This personal remark is very true. Hegel's abominable style was compensated by external numbers, letters, and subdivisions, which make matters only worse!)

§38

(Editor's note: This § number is missing. I have put it in and filled it with remarks on the beginning of logic from Hegel's Logic, W IV, p. 69-80.)

Only recently the difficulty in finding a beginning in philosophy has been stressed. The reason for this difficulty, as well as the possibility of solving it, has been much discussed. It is supposed that the begin-

---

* Here follows the "famous" passage: Logic describes the thought of God before the creation of the world. This mythical image and religious phrase sounds, of course, ridiculous in a sober logical context.

ning of philosophy must be either mediate or immediate; it is easy to show that it can be neither one
nor the other, thus refuting either approach. True,
the principle of any philosophy also expresses a beginning, but this beginning is objective and not subjective; it is the beginning of all things. The principle
is a content somehow determined—water, the One,
nous, idea, substance, monad, and so forth; or, where
it relates to the nature of cognition—like thought,
intuition, sensation, ego, or subjectivity itself—it still
begins with content. A subjective beginning in the
sense of some contingent way of introducing the ex-
position is unimportant. The only important consideration is only the *question* with which philosophy
must begin: What is the truth and the absolute basis
of all things?

The need of philosophy to begin with its own
question is denied by dogmatists, who seek a dem-
onstration of their principle; by skeptics, who seek
a subjective criterion with which to meet dogmatic
philosophy; and by those who begin with explosive
abruptness from their inner revelation, faith, intellectual intuition, and the like, and desire to dispense
with method and logic.

To begin the beginning with a chosen content is
to begin with an abstraction. The difficulty in this
approach is this: In its development thought is forced
to regard itself, the behavior of cognition, every bit
as much as the content on which it reflects. *Subjective activity is grasped as an essential moment of
objective truth, necessitating the uniting method with
content, and form with principle.* There is nothing
in Heaven, Nature, Spirit, or anywhere else, which
does not contain immediacy as well as mediacy, so
that these two determinations are seen to be unsepa-
rated and inseparable.

Any and every immediacy is what it is in distinction from the mediated; it is always at every moment
simply that which it is in opposition to all complex-

ity. As such it is a Being pure and simple; it is Being and nothing else, without any further determination or filling. Being is here the beginning, represented as arising from the negation of mediation. To begin on the subjective side with pure being is to begin in abstraction from all specific and complex content of finite knowledge. Nothing is considered except the decision (which might appear arbitrary) to consider thought as such. Abstracted from all presuppositions and mediations, thought has no foundation except itself. Further, immediate being is thus also the *thought* of immediacy as it cannot hold in itself any such determination relative to another—the latter would be differentiation and mutual relation, and thus mediation. The beginning therefore is pure thought *and* Being.

Beginning is the beginning of something and not of nothing, namely of that which begins in and with it; it cannot hold on to its immediacy. Thus consciousness is led back on its road from immediacy, with which it begins, to absolute knowledge as its inmost truth; and the first term, which entered the stage as the immediate, arises, precisely, from this last term, the foundation. What is essential is not so much that a pure immediate is the beginning, but that the Absolute in its totality, forms a cycle returning upon itself, wherein the first is also last, and the last first. This consideration is of essential importance, as will be more clearly evident in the logic itself.

In order to appease those who are dissatisfied with "being" as the beginning of logic, we could omit being as the beginning. Then the only requirement would be to make a pure beginning. Nothing but beginning is left and it would remain to be seen what that is, for, so far, there is nothing but an immediate beginning as something which is to begin. The beginning is not pure nothing; it is a nothing from which something is to proceed; being is already

99

contained in the beginning. In other words, the beginning contains both, being and nothing; it is the unity of both—not-being which is being, and being which is also not-being.

Further, on the one hand being and nothing are present in the beginning as distinct from one another: The beginning points to something other; it is not-being related to being which is to be. That which is beginning, as yet is not, it is advancing toward being. The beginning therefore contains being as having this characteristic. It stems from and transcends not-being, as its opposite. On the other hand the beginning is the undifferentiated unity of that which is beginning to be and equally, as yet, is not. The opposites, being and not-being, are in immediate in the beginning. The analysis of the beginning thus yields the concept of the unity of being and not-being, or the unity of the state of being differentiated and of being un-differentiated, or the identity of identity and non-identity.

If anyone, impatient of the consideration of the abstract beginning, should demand that we begin, not with the beginning, but directly with the subject-matter itself, the answer is that the task is to discover what this subject-matter is. The Science must not presuppose this as known.

If any form is taken for the beginning in preference to empty being, then the beginning suffers from the flaws mentioned. Those who remain dissatisfied with this beginning are asked to set themselves the task of beginning differently and yet avoid these faults.

QUALITY

§39

Pure *Being* is simply what it is; it is at the same time pure thought, identity. This self-sameness of Being is the beginning definition of the Absolute; Being begins, beginning is.

In representational thinking something is substituted for Being. In turn, Being is predicated of the substitute. For instance, in religious thinking, it is said: God is the sum total of all realities; or, God is the Being in all existing beings. Or, non-religious thinking turns to the choice of various first principles: The absolute I am I, the absolute indifference, intellectual intuition, truth, certainty, etc. All such beginnings of philosophy actually begin with Being as defined above, although they all mix it with intuitive or otherwise mediated contents.

The main defect of all representational thinking is that the identity of Being is *not a* predicate of any presupposed object.

§40

The second definition of the Absolute follows from this pure "not." Pure Being is also pure "not." The identity of Being in all beings precludes its identity with any or only one of them. The Absolute negates all things that are not absolute. It is their Nothing or negativity. The Absolute pervades all finite and definite positions; ruling out the metaphysical value of positivisms, and thereby affirming its sovereign *freedom*. It is unutterable, unpredictable (unsagbar).

Nonetheless this negativity or freedom of the Absolute can be abstractly isolated or representationally pictured. For Religion, then: God is the supreme Being beyond all determinations; or the Void which is neither definite nor indefinite. Or, object metaphysics pictures the Absolute as a thing-in-itself without form or content. Or, sometimes, compromisers try to save a part of Being from its all-pervasive negativity, for example by postulating the conservation of matter in all changes.

Logical reflection transcends any one aspect of the Absolute that is posited as final. This process of further and more concrete self-determinations of the Absolute has a necessity which is logical as well as ontological.

§41

Being is One in its self-identity as well as in its creative negativity; it is the unity of identity and non-identity, rationality and irrationality. And *this* ontological unity is Being as *Origin;* it unites being and nothing. Being as origin proceeds from the beginning to that of which it is the beginning, but which it is not yet. Whatever is to be, is not; but its beginning to be originates its real possibility. Its non-being in its beginning contains potentially its being.

The ordinary object-image represents the Origin as a spatial-temporal becoming, a change of waxing and waning, of appearing and disappearing, of something which is done and undone. If this object-image of becoming is analyzed, it must be admitted that it is *one* representation and that even this formal-logical concept presupposes the ontological categories of being and nothing as inevitable opposites. It is just as necessary and true to distinguish them, as it is to unite them as inseparable; together they originate the concrete identity of what comes to be there (Dasein).

104

It does not require much wit to poke fun at the proposition that Being and Nothing are One; as if it were one and the same to me whether the air and the sun, or my city and its law, or God were something or nothing. Such thoughtless foolishness stems from practical utilitarian interests from which the existence and nonexistence of a good thing is of vital importance; and from the representational object-thinking which reigns in all sciences, but not in philosophy.

Philosophy, on the contrary, emancipates man from the dominance of an infinite multitude of finite intentionalities.

§42

That which has come out of its *origin* contradicts the immediacy of the origin; but is, in turn, as immediate as the origin. This concrete contradiction of immediacy and mediation is there; it is the *present moment* (Dasein), and all present moments. Being is *omnipresence*.

The Absolute is simply there in every material or ideal, temporal or non-temporal reality. It is the origin of its presence and of its absence. In every moment it balances being and nothing, beginning and unbeginning, arising and vanishing. It is determined to be there and not to be there. It steps forth in simple unity with itself, but cannot arrest its step.

Zeno and the ancients realized the dialectic of the moment, but only negatively. The One, the Absolute, was neither arising nor vanishing. They failed to see its presence in all arising and vanishing moments.

§43

Being at every moment is qualitatively or individually determined. It constantly determines itself anew at each step. It utters or spends itself but also remains itself in all qualitative changes. This qualitative self-determination of Being in each decision constitutes *reality* (Realität). It is one and other than one, or many moments. It relates itself to itself through this "othering" or constant self-alteration of its moments. This being for themselves is inseparable from their being for others—all are in the same situation.

§44-46

Reality presents a breadth of present moments internally related to themselves and externally related to each other. It is externalized if its otherness is thought in abstraction from its internal relation. In this its *self-alienation* it consists of entities (Etwas) which have qualities; and they, in turn, are entities external to the entity which has them. This is the contingent realm of endless relativities. This self-estrangement belongs to and characterizes reality. (Hegel's ontological basis for his philosophy of nature.)

Atomistic philosophy is the standpoint in which the Absolute is determined as many ones which are indifferent to each other and happen by accident (Zufall). To be other and other at each existing moment characterizes all external realities. This qualitative determination and their accidental relativity is their own real contradiction; it renders them *finite* and *unstable*.

§47

In an endless cycle finite realities are posited and cancelled. This is a bad or irrational *endlessness*. The finite, although it can never last, always recurs and posits and holds on to itself. The finite shall not remain in its finitude, yet is incapable of true infinity. It is merely the perennial contradiction or dissatisfaction with itself that it wants and does not want to be finite. This progression *ad infinitum* expresses the dialectic of the finite one-and-other—a realm of care, futility, and sorrow.

§48

Every one is also the other of another and vice-versa. If this mutual alienation is comprehended, Being negates its negation and thereby affirms itself as the one in the other. It then remains itself in all changes and transition. This is *true infinity* of Being. All otherness is both in it as well as for it. It is Being in and for itself. (Sections 49-51 are unintelligible to me; they contain a transition to the second part of the Logic, entitled Quantity.)

QUANTITY

§52

The Absolute is pure *quantity*. The quantitative determination of Being presupposes its qualitative self-determination wherein it is one with itself; at the same time quantity disregards its own presupposition, and is indifferent to it. Thus, increase or decrease of quantitative magnitudes of extension or intensity does not necessarily change the quality; for example, the color red may cover a large or a small area or may be a strong or a weak red, but still it remains the color red.

The indifference of quantitative thinking to qualitative differences may result in *reductionism:* For materialism everything is reduced to matter with no regard for the living differentiations of forms. Another example would be the reduction of all bodies to pure extension.

§53

Quantity is the concrete contradiction of *discreet* units and *continuous* unity. Each is its own opposite: The discreet unit is a unit of a continuous whole; continuity is the unity of many discreet units.

This dialectic underlies the antinomies of space, time, and matter. Are they beginning and ending, or unbeginning and unending; are they infinitely divisible or indivisibly whole? Such questions are abstract either/or questions of reason.

Dialectically the same whole is the concrete contradiction of its own necessary attributes of discreet-ness and continuity: The Absolute is at once temporal *and* eternal.

§54

Quantity exists essentially as *quantum* or magnitude. The quantum is a unit of quantity. One unit is essentially limited by another unit (das Eins). Every self-limitation is also a self-transcendence; every "one," by excluding an "other," is defining itself as exclusive of the "other." It is also the "other" of the "other."

§55

Numbers are units of quantity completely determined by the law of their series. As many discreet "ones" they are a multitude; as continuous they are a unity. The whole quantum is at once number, multitude, and unity.

§56

Number as *extensive* magnitude is limited merely within quantity; as *intensive* magnitude or degree it is, in addition to this, limited by non-quantitative determinations of Being. It is external and indifferent to that which it measures.

§57

Quantum as extensive magnitude or as intensive degree reveals the *real contradiction* implicit in quantity: As concept, each quantity is the same identity, regardless how many times it is repeated; as absolute externality or pure form of all perceptions and percepts, each quantity is not identical, but equal to, or more or less than, any other quantity. This dialectic makes possible the mathematical quantitative progression and regression of adding and subtracting and of multiplying and dividing (§197).

§58

The real contradiction of the quantum is its onto-logical quality; it is the *dialectical unity of quantita-tive form and non-quantitative content.*

§59-60

Measure is the real process which calculates the quantitative aspect of all things as immediately tied up with their qualitative changes (§52).

§61

The correlation of increases or decreases of the quantum with qualitative changes does not cancel their distinction; they remain opposites in spite of and within their correlation.

§62

Quality determines quantity, and quantity deter-mines quality. This is a mutual, unsettled, dynamic *fluctuation* and unrest. Measure as this dynamic proc-ess is not only a static well-balanced harmony, a "nothing too much," but also immense or measure-less (masslos).

§63

The rational process of measuring Being is there-fore also an irrational endlessness. This struggle is ontologically justified; it is grounded in the dialectic of Being itself. Being itself tries to determine itself as quantity without ever achieving this completely. It is opposed to itself in itself. Such a unity of necessary opposites reveals the dialectical *essence* (Wesen) of Being.

(The German word *Wesen* means: Essential condition of a living state of affairs, intrinsic value or core of character, the constitutional organization of reality. Hegel uses Wesen in all these meanings.)

ESSENCE

§64

The Absolute is Essence. It distinguishes essential contradictions or polarities within itself while maintaining its concrete identity in this activity. This is its own dialectic, not an external reflection which *we* make about it. Being posits the negation of itself as real; what *seems* to be also is. This is the ontological foundation of the subject-logic (Begriff) of truth and illusion: If illusion is known to be illusion, it is known in truth.

§65

Essential being is an internal relation of its own opposites to itself. Being relates back into itself what seems foreign to itself. Being as essence is this *mediation of seeming and being*. (Hegel uses expressions which are linguistically impossible, for example, "Reflexion des Seins in sich.")

§66

The Absolute is *concrete* identity. That is, an identity of and through all differences of which it is the identity. As essential, these differences are concrete universals, essential dimensions, or realms of Being.

The formal identity of reason is the same identity, but abstracted from its manifold content. Disregarding differences, rationalism contains them only in the simple, general forms to which they are reduced. Parts of the concrete whole are either left out, or they are formulated as a generalization inclusive of their common features, but exclusive of their differences. Either is equally accidental and arbitrary.

Reason fails to understand the Absolute as concrete identity taking it in abstraction from the world. For reason and rationalism, "absolute" is equivalent to "abstract." Formal logic expresses its abstract identity as *general law of thought:* Everything is identical, A is A; negatively, A cannot be both A and non-A. These laws of reason are not laws of comprehension, but are comprehended within it. Identity moves from a first A to the second A, which thus is not identical with the first. A is identical with A only in abstraction from movement. It cannot state itself without a non-identical difference.

The second proposition, the law of non-contradiction, contradicts itself by contradicting contradiction.

§67

Every dialectical negation relates real opposites, which may be distinct, different, contrary, or contradictory. Negation thus posits what it excludes. The Absolute differentiates itself and mediates itself to itself through its own *negativity* (§40).

When the real opposites of dialectic are stated in formal-logical propositions, they become ordinary, formal-logical contradictions. For example: Everything is identical *and* different, becomes "Everything is identical" contradicts "Everything is different."

§68

In every distinguishing situation, each pole is for itself that which it is; it also is not for itself what it is, but only in contrasting relation to that which it is not. If this *relativity* is rejected, each pole *seems* to be independent.

69

Everything is *different;* there are no two things in reality that are exactly alike (§43). The many are the many of a One; the One is the One of its many members. For many to be simply many would be a meaningless, analytical tautology, saying the same thing twice. In formal logic the principle of difference contradicts the principle of identity. For dialectic one principle is just as essential as the other. Or again, mathematical quantitative thought compares the many in their external difference. Many magnitudes are compared as being equal or unequal. But equation does not eliminate the essential difference of universals.

For dialectic *internal difference* is as important as *external difference;* both are essential universals.

Being distinguishes itself, from itself, in itself. This essential identity must not be confused with equational comparative relations of equal and unequal magnitudes.

The essential self-differentiation of Being relates its universals as *negative* and *positive,* as position and opposition. The position is *not* what its opposition is; but it also is what it is by its opposition to the opposition. The opposition is *not* what the position is; it is what it is by its opposition to the position. Each negates its own negation and thereby posits or affirms itself.

The formal-logical law of the excluded middle—A must either be affirmed or denied—is comprehended in the essential dialectical affirmation: By excluding that which is not A from A, it establishes

A through its negation. But reason does not comprehend comprehension and thinks, in its peculiar thoughtlessness, that the law of the excluded middle or formal-logical exclusion is splendid in its isolation.

§72

Position and opposition contain both their *mutual affirmation and negation* in themselves. Each finds itself in its opposed other—A becomes (Ab), B becomes (Ba). The essential Being in each is thus Being in and for itself. Position and opposition perish as independent entities and thus they reach their common ground, their identical essence. (zu Grunde gehn means both—it does not mean "fall to the ground" as some "translations" have it.)

§73

Everything is grounded in this unity of identity and non-identity, of one and other, of sameness and distinction, of affirmation and negation. The Absolute is essentially dialectical. Dialectic is the essence of Being or Being as *essence*. Essence is the *sufficient ground* of all that seems to be non-absolute or finite. A is non-A: The Absolute maintains itself in that which seems to escape it.

§74

There is nothing that is not mediated. But totality of mediation simply and immediately is. The immediate presence of mediation is *existence*. (§43)

Because the essential ground is the same in all existences, it leaves them indeterminate or free: (§40): Good as well as evil actions, efficiency or inefficiency, one set of consequences or another, are all sufficiently grounded in the essence of being.

120

So a good reason or ground may be found for everything; everything can be rationalized. Because there is a sufficient ground for everything in general, it is insufficient for anything in particular.

§75

This unity of the *all-determining ground* and *indeterminacy* is a real contradiction. If it is fixed and isolated as such, it is pictured as thing-in-itself in relation to things of experience. On the one hand the things of experience are the appearances of the thing in itself; on the other hand they are left undetermined by it.

§76

In other words, Being *has* qualities; it does not hold itself responsible for them. To *have* is not to *be*. Nevertheless to *have* qualities which have become problematic means to *be* problematic. Being is a problem to itself.

§77

Essential qualities of Being are general matters like electricity or magnetism in nature, or economics and politics in history. In reason they are separated from an underlying substratum in which they are grounded but not identified. Being, then, is an enigma, a riddle, a problem to itself. This is the essential, *problematic world-view of reason.*

§78-80

General definite objects of various sciences *seem* thus to have escaped from the dialectical Essence of all Being, which is their ground. From the point of view of their unrelated manyness, Being is a vague unessential background, a "first matter" of which they are the essential forms. From the point of view of their grounding unity, they are many material manifestations of a non-material, universal form. *Appearance* is thus a unity of form in many general items or one material world differently formed. The distinction of *essential* and *unessential* enacts the very dialectical Essence which seems to have been denied.

§81

Essence must appear. It appears as *existence* (§74). Essence does not exist outside, or apart of, or behind, or beyond its existential appearance.

§82

Existence is the immediately appearing unity of immediacy and mediation, of being and seeming to be, of essential and non-essential, of being unproblematic in being problematic.

§83

Existence is a *being in and for itself*. A is what it is for itself by not being B; B is what it is for itself by not being A. Each and all existences enact together the same dialectical unity of oposites; they are *dependent* and *independent* in their *interdependence*.

§84

Independent existences are dependent members of an existential situation and process. One member is nothing outside the struggle with another member;

the whole *struggle* is nothing apart from the members engaged in it.

§85

Being is essentially *Life*. It could not do what it does—behave dialectically—were it a dead, inert mass-mechanism and not alive. Life utters or manifests itself in all of its functions which are expressions of its power.

Physically, this power appears in attraction and repulsion; *love* and *strife*, interlocked, organize the living world, from solar systems to minute organisms. This process of self-division and self-integration of the organic whole is infinite, but each step in it is finite. Insofar as one finite condition is brought about by other previous conditions, it both is and is not rationally determined; determined insofar it could not have come to pass without real antecedents, undetermined or irrational as its newness is not conditioned by its antecedents.

Life is rational *and* irrational.

§86

Living centers of power appear to each other as strangers. By this mutual estrangement they are given to each other externally or physically. Something is "physical" means it is a given to another.

Souls distinguish their own functions from themselves; at the same time they hold themselves responsible for their activity. In being thus responsible, and holding others responsible in the same sense, their physical bodies are interpreted as expressions of souls.

Soul and body, hence, are the internal actuality and the external aspect of the same living whole.

123

§87

Life insists on living in this contradiction of self-recognition and self-estrangement, of inner essence and outer appearance; this is its essential *existence*.

§88

Physical appearance of life is life itself in the form of given externality. Only life can thus appear to itself. There is nothing in the appearance of life that does not manifest its essential existence; likewise there is no essential existence that does manifest itself to others. Life is *self-manifestation*.

§89

These two sides of life can be abstractly separated into a psycho-physical *dualism* wherein the externally given, the appearing body of life, is nothing but a dead husk; and the internal actuality of life, separated from its objective embodiments, is but irrational subjectivity. Materialism is as one-sided and deficient as psychism.

§90

Life is active out of itself, in itself and for itself. This concrete identity is its *actuality* (Wirklichkeit). Only that which acts is actually real or alive.

§91

Actuality is the unity of essence and existence, of the inner world of life and the outer world of its appearance. The essence of Being is the dialectical unity of its opposites; present in the self-knowledge of Being, it becomes conscious actuality. Actual existence participates thereby in this essence and expresses its dialectic in its activities.

§92

Actuality is the power to do or to decide what it is going to be or not to be. This is actuality in the mode of potentiality or possibility. Only that which becomes actual is really possible; what is not actualized is thereby rendered impossible.

This *ontological modality of real possibility* is not the "possible" as defined in the subjective thinking of sciences—some abstract generality that may or may not be verified by experiments; the results of which remain more or less probable.

§93

Chance or contingency is the moment of decision, wherein actuality decides what it is or is not going to be, taken in its immediacy.

§94

In this moment everything seems to be possible, though this moment is an abstraction from and in actuality. The actualized content in which the decision terminates in turn decides the *objective worth or worthlessness of the decision.*

§95

The moment of decision is the condition of that which it makes actual; but in retrospective relation to the actualized content, it is a mere presupposition which is in turn conditioned by that which has become actual.

(For example, the Elizabethan Age was the condition making Shakespeare possible; but the actual Shakespeare renders this condition *his* environment. It would not be that without reference to his actuality.)

This mutual interdependence of action and reaction is the interplay of conditions conditioning each other. Every action is a reaction, every reaction is an action. Their totality is the *necessity* of actuality; it is impossible for it not to be the totality of all its interactivities.

This absolute identity of actuality and necessity is *substance*. It maintains itself as One in the interplay of its actualities. Substance posits, cancels, and preserves them in all their real modalities. Any momentary actuality in its immediacy or in abstraction from substance is *accidental*.

Substance is the absolute power and fullness of *value* (Reichtum) in all its contents; it is the unity of necessity and free creativity. Apart from its full manifestation and actuality, substance would be nothing but indifference against all differences of life.

Substance is *sufficient Cause*. It ties all actualities back to its own power. It is thus the universal connection of all things.

Cause posits actual existences. Compared to its plentitude, they are accidental or contingent. Cause, however, also cancels out the contingencies of existence but preserves them in its own necessary and eternal process.

Original *infinite creativity* and the finite creature

are absolute opposites. Yet, since the original Cause (Ur-Sache) is nothing apart from that which it creates, they are opposites in a negative relation, or relative opposites. The Absolute is both opposed to itself and united with itself.

Cause is fully actualized in its effects. There is no form, content, or shape of life that does not flow from the creative universal source of creativity. Further, on the one hand, Cause is also limiting itself when it bestows independent reality to interdependent creatures. On the other hand, it cancels its own self-limitation. By negating its own self-negation, it returns to itself and restores its wholeness. In short, the Absolute is actual in its creations, actual in their annihilation and actual in preserving them in its eternal life.

Dualism keeps the absolute and the relative, the infinite and the finite, apart. Either side is thus a meaningless abstraction (see §48). The finite creature apart from infinite creation is nothing; just as infinite creation apart from that which it creates is nothing.

In empirical sciences causality is a formal relation of given contents. The search for such causal relations leads only to a partial determination of contents, and since partial determination is also partial in-determination, the scientific struggle to determine what ought to be determined, but never can be completely determined is an endless progression and regression of partial antecedents and consequences.

§102-106

The true nature of cause and effect has turned out to be a circular movement of reciprocal action. As conscious of itself it is the subject which makes itself its own object. It reveals itself as subject-object which is the *Concept* (Begriff).

Substance is subject: Subject is substantial when

127

it dedicates itself to the fullness and objective necessity of actuality; substance is subjective when it affirms its necessity as its own will and *freedom*.

§107

The Concept is *self-knowledge* and living actuality. It distinguishes essential opposites, thinks their actual reciprocity, and is their ontological-logical, conscious identity.

§108

The Concept thus unites essence in *truth*. Dialectical essence of all Being knows itself and becomes true in and for itself.

All ontological categories developed thus far are also categories of the subject thinking them as its own. The ontological identity of being with itself, from which we started, is also a logical aspect of the Concept.

The ontological-logical movement is an ever deeper concentration of Being introscending into itself, progressing from less perfect to more perfect revelation of its dialectical nature. In the Concept, Being reaches its innermost freedom in overcoming necessary but one-sided views of itself. In realizing their imitations, they are transcended and preserved.

To enhance freedom by reducing and integrating its restrictions is the true meaning of life. Restrictive positions become presuppositions for higher levels, as scales on a ladder.

The Concept—this actual subject-object in process of self-realization—must restore its integrity out of its self-alienations in which it seems lost. It must mediate its immediacies in order to maintain its balance. What is usually called concept is a dead generality without freedom and life. This is the case because abstract reason ignores imperfections in its perfect and exact classes. In the dialectical Concept, however, the dialectical essence of Being is contracted into a new meaning of immediacy. It simply is and exists in its actuality. It freely mirrors a universe in itself. In thinking that which is—in all its hardness and inevitability—the Concept remains at peace and in agreement with itself.

Freedom and self-hood, the full reconciliation of subject and object is reached when the self dedicates itself to the substantial contents and values of the world. This is not a flight from its negativity or an escape from unavoidable problems and contradictions; it is an elevation above and liberation from narrowness.

The Concept is the unity of necessity and freedom. Man, having reached his Concept, cannot possibly will not to be free; this impossibility is the negative statement of necessity. He is destined to be free. Truth sets him free and only in freedom can he pursue truth.

THE CONCEPT

§109

The *Concept* (Begriff) grasps and focuses in itself the essential dialectic of Being. Like Being, it determines itself in and for itself; unlike Being, it knows this to be the case. It is thus both substantial and consciously free, an actual totality of affirmations and negations, a living mirror of the universe (Reflexion des Wesens in sich!). It is the identity of subject-object knowing itself as such.

The Concept is the *essence of personality*.

§110

The Concept matures in a process of spiritual growth. Its *freedom* grows as it actively appropriates necessary and substantial contents of the world. As it opens itself to the world, the world discloses itself in it. Such is the two-way movement of freedom.

§111

Subjective appropriation and *objective content* are dialectical opposites in and of the Concept; it is thus at once "subject-object." Truth exists for itself in the Concept and nowhere else. Or, truth is the known presence of the ontological dialectic in the subject.

Forms or shapes (Gestalten) of the Concept, woven into a living spiritual texture, constitute actuality (Wirklichkeit). Actuality, therefore, does not coincide with the more abstract category of reality

(§43) of whatsoever occurs or is given. The task of the logic of the Concept is to examine the value and validity of its concrete forms—a task hitherto but rarely tackled in the history of logic.

Being and Essence are dialectical in themselves; in addition, they are dialectical in and for the Concept—they resemble the Concept (in welchem sie scheint!). In themselves they are not concentrated in the uniqueness of free persons. In and for the Concept, they are seen as its own universal aspects: It participates in Being and Essence and they participate in it. Forms of the Concept, thus, are not to be mistaken for the forms in the sense of formal logic. The latter forms are dead, ineffectual, non-actual containers, indifferently consuming anything that is thrown to them; even though formal logic as a whole is itself one of actual forms of the Concept.

§112

The actual Concept effects itself; it is the *cause of itself*.

As participating in the identity of Being with itself (§39), it is *universal;* as participating in essential opposites or contrary spheres of Being, it is *particular* (§71); as unique self-determination, which realizes for itself what it is in itself or as actualizing its potentiality, it is *individual.* Thus there is no life or actuality in general: Its life is its universality, which is through and through individuated (§43), and individuation fully caught up in universality.

§113

The Concept as actual in the unique unity of universality, particularity, and individuality is the same in all persons. I am what thou art: Another to thee; thou art what I am: Another to me. This is the *concrete identity* of the Concept.

I am what we all are; we all are what I am. This is *concrete universality* of the Concept. The dialectical meeting of I and thou unites the concrete identity and the concrete universality of the Concept in one and the same living universe of discourse.

The Concept does not leave any of its members outside itself, as the rational concept does.

When this comprehensive meaning of Concept as actual is understood, it is manifestly clear that the empirically concrete is a weak analogy of the concreteness of the Concept. For the former, many external items are held together by an equally external form; for example, the concept of an empirical house is a generalized object-image (Vorstellung). Herein concepts are abstracted both from the universality of Being and from unique individuals. The saying that concepts are only abstract is quite valid for empirical generalizations.

In contrast, in the concreteness of the Concept, *each person honors the other as differently and uniquely representing the same Absolute.*

§114

The Judgment (Ur-Teil) is the incessant activity of *self-criticism*, whereby the Concept manifests its own universality, particularity, and individuality; it is the aboriginal (ursprünglich) self-distinction of subject, making itself its own object, of and within its concrete unity. (Hegel takes the current "Urteil" —judgment in the ordinary sense of a proposition, S is P—and interprets it in the original root-meaning of the word, "aboriginal partition," never thought of in the ordinary usage.)

Propositions of reason, in contrast, are not such concrete self-distinctions. They isolate the universal as an abstract generality; subsume a particular class under it, and co-ordinate particular classes as species of the same genus; and treat the individual as a case

of its species. Reason fixes and affixes general marks
by which the subjective thinking of psychology gropes
around and finds its way in its irrational (begrifflos)
experience. It distinguishes concepts as clear when
they belong to a genus; as distinct when they are
known as co-ordinated species of the same genus.
The opposites of Essence—contraries and contradic-
tories, affirmations and negations—are likewise for-
malized and deprived of life.

§115

Life and spirit exist in the ever-renewed *effort*
to hold their different levels of universality, particularity, and individuality together; this is the "Judgment" as constant alertness and self-criticism. The
Judgment corrects temptations to exist in one direction or level of actuality at the expense of other
levels. It unites individual and universal life, mediated by spheres of essential opposites.

In reason the actual subject becomes a formal S
in a proposition; the particular sphere becomes a
general P (predicate) of a proposition; and the universal becomes a formal copula "is" which indifferently links anything with anything. Reason thus
caricatures Comprehension.

In the actual Concept, universal, particular, and
individual concerns form a living whole of opposites.
The subject as agent is not merely an indefinite X
which *has* qualities; rather it *is* in and through its
opposite functions and is responsible or accountable
for them (§76).

§116

The *ontological self-distinction* (Ur-Teil) is prior
to the formal-logical julgment. The Absolute differentiates its universality and its individuation, mediating them through essential spheres of life. Univer-

sality and individuality are distinguished and united in this same process of the absolute "Judgment" (Ur-Teil).

The ordinary judgment subsumes something given under a general object-image (Vorstellung); it is more or less correct or incorrect. It is still logical in that it is responsible for its correctness; it must answer yes or no.

Below the formal-logic judgments are irrational expressions of private-subjective, merely psychical or mental states which do not claim truth, but express only immediate personal feelings, wants and the like.

§117

The Concept in its *immediate finitude* appears as a psycho-physical organism. Though the physical body and the functioning soul may be studied as if they were different entities, when abstractly separated by reason, in actuality the body is the appearing and external aspect of the soul. Apart from this dialectical concreteness of the appearing subject-object or Concept, both sides vanish; The object-side becomes unknowable; the subject-side has no objective embodiment.

§118-128

(These paragraphs deal with the logical distinctions of judgments. They are divided into analytic and synthetic. The synthetic is divided into singular judgments which relate this subject S with a general predicate, P; particular judgments do the same for groups of finite things; and general judgments make general statements about general classes of such things.

The philosophical conclusion is this: Reason is a concrete process and *struggle of the finite subject with its own otherness, the finite object*. This struggle

to subject the obstreperous "other" to logical forms—
to appropriate them in sciences—ought to go on
although it can never achieve its end.

The struggle of the rational will with the irrational "positive" or given, is as a whole process a
form of speculative truth; or in Kantian language, a
form of the synthesis a priori.)

§129

Self-distinction (Ur-Teil) is the process whereby
the Concept (Begriff) actualizes its own concrete
identity: Reciprocally it is created by it. This unity
of "Concept" and "Judgment" mutually constitut-
ing one another is *Comprehension* (Vernunft).
As all-inclusive and all-conclusive, comprehensiveness (Schluss) is equivalent to the totality of Being
(§5).

All truths presuppose absolute truth as their
ground. The Absolute reveals itself as the whole
truth in the circular movement of its spheres in
which and through which movement they are moments of the same universe (§6).

Ordinarily this all-inclusive conclusiveness is
falsely referred to as syllogism (Schluss-Hegel's trick
again!); but the system of rational propositions in a
syllogism is not comprehensive and has only a faint
similarity to truth and Being. In actuality (Wirklichkeit) individuals link themselves by means of essential and contrary spheres to the whole. The Absolute
is both the ground and the goal of this sublime elevation of the finite to the infinite, and the omnipresence of the infinite in the finite.

§130

To think that the comprehensiveness of reality
and of philosophy could be demonstrated by syllogisms of reason (Verstandesschluss) is the height

of folly (begrifflos). Syllogisms merely mirror the irrationality of finite objects; they fall apart in formal subjects and general predicates indifferent to one another; they might just as well have other qualities than the ones they have. The generality under which singular subjects are subsumed is quite arbitrary; and the mediation of two terms by a third is equally arbitrary, for the relations of finite objects are external.

§131-134

(These paragraphs treat the rational syllogism, as §118-128 treated the rational proposition.) Either the *syllogism* links a singular proposition through a particular proposition to a general conclusion (s-p-g); or it links a general proposition through a singular proposition to a particular conclusion (g-s-p); or it links a particular proposition through a general proposition to a singular conclusion (p-g-s).

Aristotle discovered these three essential figures of syllogistic reasoning, but failed in his *Metaphysics* to think in the light of them. For this reason he was able to develop true Concepts of natural and spiritual realities, wherein his speculative Concept triumphs over his rationalistic descriptions of reason.

The more concrete reality is, the weaker the syllogistic statement of it. In concrete reality it is arbitrary, which of its many aspects are singled out as essential and used as linking or mediating terms. Anything may syllogistically be demonstrated and proven provided one agrees first which of the many aspects of a complex situation is to be chosen as important or necessary. In every syllogism a premise is assumed as necesary and true; even though it is a postulate of reason that each such premise, in turn, would have to be proven by another syllogism. Thus we see again the esential nature of reason as an endless progression which is just as much irrational as it is rational.

If all terms of a syllogism are quantitative, the logical copula "is" loses its logical function to identify, and becomes unimportant. Mathematical *equations* no longer determine what something is—except that they always refer to quantity; they merely compare quantities in external relations to one another. Syllogism, then, is reduced to a mathematical equation: If a first unit is equal to a second unit, and the second unit is equal to a third unit, then the third unit is equal to the first unit, and so on.

§136

Reasoning by *induction* expresses singularities in general; it formulates as an abstraction what singulars have in common. Inductive reasoning is an analogy to a syllogism, except that its postulate—singulars must have something in common—presupposes as well as yields only particular, not—truly universal classes.

Analogy is an abstract and partial identity.

§137

The whole sphere of syllogistic reasoning unsuccessfully imitates the concrete unity of the Concept; its *true concreteness contains reason as one of its abstract moments* (§13).

§138

In its necessary concatenation of propositions, reason aims to articulate *given systems:* The categorical syllogism chooses as mediating or middle term, genus and species (Gattung, Art); the hypothetical syllogism relates singular propositions through the relation of ground and consequence; the disjunctive or conjunctive syllogism mediates particular alternatives through a universal whole which is supposed to determine its members completely. Systematic reasoning thus aims at establishing the concrete Concept without realizing that it is already contained in it; it is a form of the Concept.

Reason is one form of subject-object in process. It describes itself in its own abstract terms in order to guard against its own contradictions. It thus knows itself without critical, philosophical self-comprehension. Nevertheless, as real and not abstract opposites, contradictions constitute the very life of reason.

§139

In the Concept, Being understands itself as intelligible. Thinking and Being, subject and object, are opposites in their dialectical identity. They are as inseparable as they are separable. The absolute *World-itself* is their concrete unity.

The complete speculative "Syllogism" (Schluss) mediates itself through its own dialectical negations: The absolute whole is nothing without that which it is not—nature and mind; mind is nothing apart from the background of the absolute whole and without the resistance of Nature, both of which it is not; nature is nothing apart from the whole and apart from being known in its objectivity, both of which it is not. Each of the three spheres is the intelligible Concept, the unity of subject-object, thought and Being in different modifications; each poses, opposes and presupposes the other two totalities as necessary for itself.

Anselm's *ontological argument* exemplifies the Concept or intelligibility of the Absolute as a dialectical process of self-realization of Being in the subject and of the subject in Being. He says: Certe id, quo majus cogitari nequit, non potest esse in intellectu solo. Si enim vel in solo intellectu est, potest cogitari esse et in re: quod majus est. Si ergo id, quo majus cogitari non potest, est in solo intellectu; id ipsum, quo majus cogitari non potest, est, quo majus cogitari potest. Sed certe hoc esse non potest. (It is certain that a Being, than which a greater cannot be conceived, cannot exist in the mind only. If it were in the mind only, then it could be conceived to exist beyond it; which is greater. Consequently, if that being than which a greater cannot be conceived is in the mind only, then that than which a greater can *not* be conceived, is the same as that than which a greater *can* be conceived. But certainly this cannot be so.)

Taken as a syllogism of reason, Anselm's argument is forced and faulty. The rational concept of the absolute Being as implying its existence is merely subjective and analytical. In philosophical comprehension, however, Anselm's thought is profound and true: The rational concept of the Absolute is thought as one-sided, subjective, and negative, but the breakdown (aufheben) of this subjective concept is the affirmation that the absolute Being is not one-sided, subjective, and negative. Reason, which is merely finite, is thus at once canceled as ultimate and restored in truth. The Absolute is present in this self-transcendence of the finite mind, which is also *not* self-transcendent. Being and thought are inseparably united as well as distinguished in one actuality.

Dualism only reflects on the difference: Concept is one thing, Being another thing.

Kant's critique of the ontological argument joins the same unphilosophical company which Anselm already met in Gaunilo. Just as Gaunilo remarked that one can think a perfect island whose perfection implied its existence without ever finding such an island in reality; so Kant argued that one could think the being of $100 without finding them in his pocket. The falsity and sheer subjectivity of such critism lies in its absurd clinging to some finite and given entity as if it were absolute. The error is that of thinking the Absolute or God in this manner of a given thing. This is precisely the error, that the ontological argument means to correct.

The absolute identity of being and intelligibility, or Concept, has always been at the core of all and every philosophy. Being is *logically* one with itself, which is the Concept. Concept exists *actually* and individually. Either side has the same ontological status.

Plato, Aristotle, and all their predecessors assumed this identity. Descartes and Spinoza presupposed this identity of being and intelligibility or Concept by definition or as axioms; they also illustrated it in the forms of intellectual intuition, faith, or immediate certainty. Objectivity is actual in subjects; subjectivity is objectivity real. The dialectical identity of these subject-objects is an eternal process. It is both immediately present and certain; it is also mediation and critique of all immediate certainties.

In this process, the Concept is and knows all determinations of Being as concurrently its own determinations. It produces itself in necessary, universal, original partition of itself (Ur-Teil), and is inclusive conclusiveness (Schluss) in which reason also is preserved in its abstracting function. The term for this total process comprehending itself is Idea.

(§139 concludes Hegel's logic of the Concept—but continues, nevertheless, under the same title, Concept. The fourth part of the *Logic*, however, deals with teleology, final cause, and absolute Idea. I have therefore changed the title to The Idea. In §368 and §386 Hegel himself admits that there are four, not 3, parts to his *Logic*.)

THE IDEA

§140

Logical thought begins in the *thinking* of immediate Being, in which beginning is implicit the unity of logic and ontologic. Universal Being discloses itself in the qualitative infinity of existing moments (§43). Reflecting on this result, it is found in thought that all Being is a dialectical unity of opposites. This essence of all Being discloses itself in actual existences (§91). In reflecting further again on this result, Being becomes understandable or intelligible in and for itself. As such, it is its own concept. Reflecting still further again on the movement from Being to Essence and from Essence to Concept, it is evident that the Absolute is the movement or process of self-realization, and that this process of self-realization culminates in the logic of philosophy, which is the logic of world-itself. World-totality as eternal movement in and for itself is the *absolute Idea or final cause* (Endzweck).

§141

For *objectivism,* all is object. As abstract matter it is passive: It is capable of receiving any determinations of shape or form, while also remaining indifferent towards them.

§142

The formed object is a composite or aggregate of an external manifold of general items. Their external push and pull, pressure and counter-pressure is thought in a *formal mechanism*. Measurable dif-

147

ferences are indifferent to one another; their relations are external. (Hegel's terms "mechanism" and "chemism" do not refer to particular sciences, but to metaphysical world views to which mechanics and chemists may or may not be addicted.)

§143

The object-world is a mixture of impacts of force, and resisting force by a counter-force. It is an *irrational* (begrifflos) world of violent powers (Gewalt).

§144

Either way—whether blindly acting or blindly reacting—the object is a plaything of circumstances; it is there to be pushed around and to push around in turn. This activity, which is bound to change and to corrode the object, is the *negativity* or irrationality inherent in its nature.

§145

The *absolute mechanism* is the totality of objects in attraction and repulsion. Its system comprises the partial dependence and partial independence of its members.

§146

Compared with the formal mechanism (§142), the absolute mechanism is a system of many relative gravitational systems of *attraction* and *repulsion;* all its members are oriented towards an *ideal center* or point of gravity.

§147

In all mechanisms, the differences of objects are quantitative. Yet, since there is no quantity apart from quality (§60), as measure of qualitative changes, mechanism is *chemism*.

§148

The chemical object is quantitatively determined, while remaining partly indeterminate by mere quantity. *It tends towards an equilibrium* or balance of its energies without achieving it, except momentarily (§62).

§149

To the mechanical pressures and counter pressures chemism adds qualitative determinations. Thus the chemical object constitutes itself in a *reciprocity of tensions and neutralizations,* and in organizing and binding extreme tensions into concrete wholes, it resembles living organisms.

§150

Qualitative affinities act and react upon one another in an affective continuum; their interactivity of tensions and relaxations *resembles life* and is its external image, though the chemical interactivity is not alive for itself and does not understand itself.

§151-152

In serving and *entering life,* mechanism and chemism are in continuity with it and are absorbed in its newness; they are the objective aspects of the one cosmic life.

§153

Cosmic life is qualitatively or individually determined in each of its steps; it is immediate *intentionality* (Trieb) longing to express and embody itself. Purpose (Zweck) directs living impulses and produces shape and form. It is a concrete universal, creating and holding its many qualities or functions within its identity. Mechanism and chemism are its external aspects or appearances. Life, individually organized, must view other lives equally organized from the outside. The physical appearance is the appearing estrangement of life in and for itself. Purpose is, on the contrary, the Concept life has in and for itself in process and in activity: It is the inner functional reality of mechanism and chemism. That which it is "in itself," potentially, (an sich).

The concepts of reason are incompetent to think purpose; their abstract generality always misses every concrete decision. Reason, from the point of view of the absolute comprehensiveness and absolute individuation of teleological life, is irrational and uncomprehending (begrifflos, unvernünftig). Reason and rationalism, therefore, favor mechanism because the external descriptions are abstracted from life-content and value.

Teleological life is always in the making. It lives in an anticipation of what it should become. *This ought (sollen) itself is;* it exists in an inevitable moment in the dialectical movement of all life.

§154-155

For reason, ends and means fall apart; they are external to one another. In the immediacy of reason, purpose is finite. Everything is treated as means to momentary ends. Objects are supposed to be there only to serve one's pleasure and profit.

As a world-view, this standpoint is a rationalistic teleologism in which every end may become a means, and every means may become an end, which amounts to an absurd endlessness.

Against this finite teleology, Kant has restored the *Idea of Life:* In his *Practical Reason,* he discovered and justified the self-determination of the good will. In its form of universality, the will represents the Absolute and is therefore never merely a means to an external end. This is the *Concept of inner purposiveness.*

In his stress on the formal universality of the will, however, he missed Aristotle's concept of the concrete teleology of life, in which all functions serve each other mutually as ends and means in the self-realization of the whole. Every function of the soul is a means of the whole which could not be what it is without it, and the whole is a means whereby each function is mediated. This is true infinity of purpose (§48).

This inner organic teleology is infinitely superior to the external teleologism of the recent enlightenment period. (What Hegel says against its philistine complacency holds equally for the no less philistine American *pragmatism,* for which truth is that which works for me, reality is the sum total of all my expectations, and thought is nothing but the phase of a profitable action)

§156

Purposive activity unites subjective ends and objective means in such a way that the latter completely expresses or embodies the former (pen, ink, and paper, for example, are means without which there would be no book as expression of my desire and purpose to write it).

§157

The Concept in *purposive activity and process is the final cause* or absolute Idea. It could not realize itself without the mechanism and chemism of the world which it transfigures into participants of its meaningful activity.

§158

Using material objects and their blind powers, letting them serve purposes not their own, but nevertheless working in and for purpose, is the *cunning of comprehension* (List der Vernunft).

Comprehensive purposiveness is not identical with the material processes which it pits against each other; nevertheless it is consuming them and is their concrete unity bestowing cohesion to them (railroads, locomotives, coaches, signal systems, etc., are a heap of dead meaningless materials outside of and apart from purposive activity of commerce and travel which they serve).

§159-160

Hypothetical subjective ends and external means are thus comprehended in an objective purposiveness; it forms particular systems of life, in which ends and means are aspects of one complete purpose (in my example: It makes little difference to the whole railroad system which passenger is moved by which vehicle, or which agent has sold him which ticket). Objective purposiveness is thus a self-determining, intelligible whole of subjective activities. In contrast to subjective ends and means, this self-determining purposive whole does not make the distinction of what it should be and what it is: The means by which it is realized are fully absorbed in its process.

Intelligible objectivity and *objective intelligibility* in process are particular expressions of the Idea.

§161

All previous determinations of the Absolute are absorbed in this definition: *The Absolute is Idea.* They all participate in its truth and are true only as far as they participate in it.

Every single being has barriers, and is determined by one particular aspect of itself or another. Each aspect needs other aspects. In their immediacy they seem to be real in themselves, but ultimately they are real only as being mediated in the total process and inner activity of the Idea, which also constitutes the unfinality of each.

The absolute Idea is not the idea *of* something or other, rather it differentiates itself in many concrete systems of life and remains the One all-embracing process and activity in all of them.

For object-thinking finite things are real and ideas are formal-logical abstractions of reason; they start from empirical observations and are checked by referring back to them. Reason, therefore, in applying this habit of thinking to the absolute Idea, is baffled because it does not find a particular empirical starting point; it can think an idea only in the sense of an abstract generality, a generalized object-image over against its manifold content. To grasp the untruth of this standpoint of reason is the beginning of comprehension which understands why reason is one-sided and to that extent untrue.

The Idea is freedom: *The Absolute determines itself and is determined by nothing outside itself. Its eternal presence is one with its restless creativity. It never stands still; it leaves standing no seemingly finished manifestations of its life.*

§162

The Idea discloses and contains in its infinite movement all dialectical correlations as its own: It may therefore just as well be called comprehensiveness (Vernunft); or unity of subject-object, identity and difference, ideal and real, infinite and finite; body and soul; or absolute possibility which necessarily brings itself into actuality; or the Absolute whose nature includes its own negation in itself, and can only be thought of as affirmations of itself; and the like. Analyzed by reason, such dialectical structures may seem formal or static; in truth they are different modifications of the absolute internal process of the Idea which eternally beholds its own creativity in the other created of itself. It infinitely divides itself (Ur-Teil) in its immense totalities—each of which participates in its independence and freedom—and withal is their transition and self-transcendence. The absolute Idea is intelligible activity, an absolute purposiveness perfectly actualized in each imperfect moment: The Final Cause.

Absolute Idea contains reason as its own analysis. Reason analyzes and readily distinguishes identity and difference, subject and object, finite and infinite, soul and body, etc. As this negative analytical function, reason is a necessary function of and within life. But when it isolates its isolating function, setting it up as a criterion of truth, reason turns into un-reason (Verstand ist Missverstand).

After setting up its abstract ideas, empty generalities, and fictitious dualisms—for example body is body and not soul, soul is soul and not body—reason vainly seeks again to unite entities which it has endowed with an illusive, seeming independence.

§163

The *individual participates* in the Idea by overcoming its abstract subjectivity and by filling itself with objective world-content; the world participates in the Idea by creating individual organs, functional subjects in and for itself. The subject thus becomes substantial, the substance becomes subjective.

§164

The *inter-penetration of universality, particularity, and individuality* in the Concept (§113) reappears in the teleological inter-penetration of individual, particular, and universal concerns and realms of life, which serve each other mutually as ends and means.

§165

Life is singular and individual; its functions are inseparable from their unique unity; they cannot be transferred, and the whole individual soul is wholly present in all its functions. It never drops out of the universe of Being. This is its *immortality*.

Life is totally different from physical "wholes" which have separable "parts." Such things are called "dead," though there is nothing dead in reality. They are abstractions; if this abstraction of dead things with a number of qualities is used to think the soul, then the soul becomes a collection of unrelated faculties. Soul and body thus fall apart like two pieces.

The true meaning of death is this, that no physical appearance and no embodiment of the soul is final or sufficient. When a finite organization of life is cancelled, its organs, the visible appearances of its functions, are dissolved in order to join other organizations of life; (as members of a club may join other clubs when the first club has out-lived its utility).

§166

The dependence of organized life on inorganic or elementary life is an inevitable deficiency and need (Mangel). In satisfying its need and in combatting its deficiency, purposive life is a perennial struggle against its *inevitable dissolution*.

§167

Every living individual is immediately this process; it is also mediated as offspring from other living individuals. The living individual not only serves itself; it also serves its kind in *procreation* and rejuvenation. In distinction from nature, the human family affirms its unity as a form of final cause.

§168

Natural life is a necessary process which reproduces individuals through their kinds and the kinds through their individuals; the kind constantly gives rise to individuals and just as constantly destroys them to maintain itself as this process.

Self-conscious life serves many kinds of causes, is aware that it does so, and may freely choose them as its own substantial values.

To give one's life to the cause of freedom is the origin of Spirit.

§169

As natural life must maintain itself by wresting its means of subsistence from the inorganic or organic life of nature, so spiritual life must gain its existence by wresting its *freedom from* the external universe; the spirit posits itself over against nature: Its labor to be *free from* nature brings about the material condition to become *free for* itself.

§170

The Idea exists in this double process of a *negative* freedom from nature and a *positive* freedom to become for itself what it is in itself.

§171

The immediate intentionality of personal existence is to appropriate the existing (Seiend) world: It is certainly uncertain about it and wants to find truth by going through an educational process in which all its certain uncertainties are explored and exploded. This desire is satisfied in philosophy. The Idea as process becomes aware of itself in philosophical knowledge. Its goal is to understand the totality of Being as a dynamic unity of opposites and to understand itself. *Ontology terminates in self-knowledge,* and *self-knowledge is ontologically significant.*

§172

Philosophical self-comprehension is beyond the boundary of reason. Reason cannot find its identity with its objects. Thus it is comprehended in philosophy. Finite knowledge known philosophically is a concrete process in which logical forms struggle forever with given non-logical contents.

§173

The method of reason is not dialectical, but *analytical.* Its concepts are formal identities and abstract generalities. Rational analysis dissolves the realities which it presupposes. It either selects one fact at the expense of the rest, or it generalizes features of the object and treats them as if they were real by themselves—empirical laws of nature. The concreteness of reality is only remembered as a vague background.

§174

True infinity absorbs finite knowledge as a necessary moment of itself; *analysis* presupposes *synthesis* (Kant defines scientific knowledge as synthesis a priori of logic, space-time, and perceptual materials;

this is one form of many syntheses a priori explored by his systematic philosophy—at least this is the Kant as Hegel sees him).

§175

Philosophy links the universality of Being, the essential particularity of its spheres and the qualitative determination of their representatives. Process in philosophy mirrors the absolute Idea.

§176

The division of philosophy is derived from emphasizing and making articulate the particular and opposed realms of Being.

§177

The philosophical method, applied to object-problems of empirical science, results in *arbitrary constructions*. The rational method of sciences, applied to philosophy, results in abstract *formalisms* ("isms").

Sciences are faced with two kinds of irrationalities: The stuff they measure and rationalize remains incommensurable and irrational (Incommensurabilitäten, Irrationalitäten); and the comprehensiveness of comprehension, which they call irrational, is more than merely rational.

§178

Because scientific knowledge is external to its objects, scientists remain irresponsible for their knowledge; and decline responsibility for the effects of knowledge in the world. In truth, however, any approach to reality characterizes reality itself. Being is present in the free attitude which the subject chooses in regard to it. The Idea as process and activity is not only actualized in knowledge, but also in the *will*.

§179

The will actualizes the purposiveness of the Idea. Its determinations and decisions determine and decide what the world is going to be. While scientific knowledge presupposes the world as given, the will transforms this given world into a task (Zweck).

The Absolute appears: As *truth* it is the *final cause* of philosophical knowledge; as *good* it is the final cause in and for all purposes.

§180

The will is a concrete *dialectical contradiction*. On the one hand, it must *know* what the object is, which it wants to transform. It must thus recognize its independent reality and adapt itself to it. On the other hand, it does not leave the object alone, but wants to influence and change it. The object is therefore both independent and not independent of the will; and the will is both dependent and not dependent on its object.

§181

This contradiction is the necessary essence of every finite will. What *ought* to be, *is* not—if the ought were fulfilled, it would cease to be an ought. That the will ought to be good shows that it is not good.

The Absolute will posits this contradiction; the will absolutely insists on existing in and as this contradiction.

But all these contradictions of finite wills express the Idea of the Good whose infinity is the perfection

159

eternally realized in and through all finite contradictions. To accept life as this dialectical struggle, eternally willed, is the final cause (End Zweck) and the good life.

§182

The absolute good is, therefore, the unity of what ought to be and what eternally is; the good coincides with the absolute truth, which is identical with the whole of reality. This dialectical identity of the truth and the good, which are two facets of the same Absolute, is the actuality of the absolute Idea in *Geist* consciously present in every man who *understands the finite in the light of the infinite.*

§183

Through the absolute idea, the finite subject in all its contradictions and failures is *reconciled* with itself and with reality.

§184

The *absolute idea makes itself available* and becomes articulate in the logic of philosophy. Method and contents are inseparable in it.

§185

The Idea is its own immediate *origin* or beginning. It is at once both individual immediacy, and universal mediation.

Seen from many abstract beginnings, the whole is a process of synthesis; the starting point is enwholed and returns to itself at *the end* when it is understood in the whole. Seen from the completed result, the logic of philosophy is a regress of analysis making explicit what is implicit in the whole.

§186

The negation of any simple beginning is not a formal contradiction, but relates the beginning, to that of which it is the beginning, or what has begun in it. This affirmative negativity is the dialectical self-differentiation (Ur-Teil) through which the idea unfolds itself. What seems to be simple and positive turns out to be complex and loaded with dialectical negations, all of which contribute to its being what it is.

§187

This universal self-differentiation of the Idea appears in many modifications. In *Being*, for example, it is one and other; in *Essence*, it is the unity of identity and non-identity or difference; in the *Concept*, it is universality and existence in personal intelligible individuation. The Idea dialectically negates all moments which are not it, and thereby affirms itself as the living soul, power and purpose of the universe.

§188

The Idea is the moving negativity of its own distinctions. In it, the *illusion* that philosophy has an *immediate beginning* disappears, together with the opposite *illusion* that its end is a *final result*.

§189

Every totality is, and expresses in itself, the movement of the Idea; the whole is whole in each and because the whole is process, there is no ultimate rest in any of its many totalities. The dialectical method is, therefore, their own method, not a formalism externally attached to them.

There is One Idea, one universe of many totalities. The idea is its own proceeding and begins for itself, what it is in itself. The speculative Idea is infinite actuality, absolute freedom, life and self-knowledge.

(The rest of this contains a transition to philosophy of nature which is unintelligible to me . . . "the Idea decides to jump into nature.")

PHILOSOPHY OF NATURE

(Hegel's philosophy of nature is admittedly weak. This weakness, however, is not due to his logic, but to his disregard of it. He has said that philosophical dialectic should not interfere with the non-dialectical formal-logical method and object problems of the sciences (§177), but now he does interfere in problems that are purely scientific.

I call these border violations a speculative fallacy —the term called "speculative" used in the usual derogatory sense; he himself calls it arbitrary construction.

Whenever a philosopher has encumbered his philosophy with sciences of his day and age, he was surely and swiftly punished; he was soon outmoded and full of dead wood. I shall cut it out as much as possible. This does not mean that there are no final findings in the sciences.)

§192-196

Nature is in itself a *living whole;* it organizes itself in *levels* of inorganic and organic appearances.

It is a mistake to suppose that the higher levels of cosmic life which appear as alive to themselves can be understood from the perspective of lower levels exclusively, where the natural life or activity is entirely unconscious. The lower levels, on the contrary, must be understood in analogy to the higher levels.

Space and *time* are categories of all perceptions and all percepts; they define and confine nature. This means that all natural processes, events, and momentary constellations of things are external to one another, replace and succeed one another.

In its immediacy, nature is therefore a realm of an all-pervasive relativity, a blind irrational flux. Everything that happens might just as well not happen, or happen differently. This is the contingency (Zufall) of all things natural.

As a living whole, nature is a total process or Idea; as contingency and externality, it is the same Idea in its otherness or self-estrangement.

If nature is defined as a system of laws—everything is as it is and not otherwise, it is eternally in order—then nature is envisaged as Idea; but since it does not know its own order, nature is the realm of a blind "must." The necessity of natural laws does not eliminate the immediate irrationality and singularity of all events through which they are actualized.

Sometimes nature has been worshipped as divine in itself (Spinoza's deus sive natura), or as the creation of God. As such, it was revered and admired for the wisdom exhibited in its complex patterns. At other times, it has been damned as defection of, or revolt against, God; or as the seed and origin of evil. Both evaluations are anchored in the dialectical unity of the Idea in its self-estrangement. So anchored, it is false to call nature evil, for evil is the internal struggle of the spirit within itself; it is a struggle of a higher reality within itself and does not pertain to the innocence of plants or the regular behavior pattern of stars.

For *external teleology* (§154), natural things are profitable or unprofitable for finite human ends; nonetheless they are, qua natural, indifferent to the use or abuse to which they are put. For this reason, external teleology does not belong to the philosophy of nature.

The active manifestations of wholeness (Idea) in nature are inferior to its conscious manifestation of the same in history, just as a living organism is inferior to the absolute spiritual organism in a work of art. The highest level of nature is reached in man, for whom a mere natural life is a living death (for example any idiotic senility). Nature in man is a potentiality for which he makes himself responsible (§170).

Philosophy of nature develops the correlation between the levels of nature and the natural sciences. The natural sciences deal in abstractions. The subject-matter of *mathematics* is nature as an ideal whole in abstraction from empirical contents; mathematics deals with the laws of its externality of space and time; mathematical *physics* investigates external appearances in abstraction from cosmic life; *physiology* studies organisms in abstraction from the organic whole of nature. As distinct from all sciences, philosophy of nature correlates these abstraction, envisaging nature as a living whole.

MATHEMATICS

§197

Kant has rightly said that space and time are pure forms of perception; every possible perception and percept is located in space and time. But he has spoiled his true theory of space and time by his idealism wherein they are regarded simply as forms of human subjectivity. Nevertheless this remains valid: Space and time are the categories which define psycho-physical nature as a material world in which everything is outside and external to every other thing, either in juxtaposition or in succession.

Space and time are infinite and continuous; they are not logical concepts. Their different stretches, units or shapes are discreet determinations within an infinite continuum, not logical classes subsumed under other logical classes. Quantity as ontological category (§53) makes mathematics possible as the science of spatial-temporal externality.

Any spatial-temporal point or unit is equal to any other, different only in location. This quantitative difference is at the same time qualitative indifference.

§198

The *dimensions* of space—high, long, deep—are arbitrary distinctions. There is no way to specify which is which, for they have but a subjective meaning: One may assume a point—for example, the center of the earth—as a point of orientation for such dimensions, but he may just as well assume any other.

§199

A *point*, on the one hand, is an infinitesimal origin of spatial configuration; on the other hand, it negates space as a whole. Geometry treats the point as positive. Thus, lines are constructed by a continuous movement of discreet points; three-dimensional figures by continuous movements of discreet planes. So constructed, pure geometric figurations are abstract and quantitative; as perceived, concrete spatial shapes are qualitative as well.

The unity of pure intuition and abstract thought renders every mathematical equation synthetic; this is the philosophical concept of mathematics. It is curious that Kant did not state this concept in general, but only exemplified synthesis by such particular examples as; A straight line is the shortest distance between two points.

(This passage is frequently misinterpreted, as if Hegel were denying Kant's synthesis or even arguing against Kant that mathematical presuppositions are analytical. Not only is this interpretation incompatible with Hegel's whole philosophy of mathematics —solidly in agreement with Kant—but the passage itself says nothing of the sort. The confusion is purely linguistic and arises from a faulty reading of "Begriff," which the interpreter understands in the ordinary sense of an abstract and analytical identity, while Hegel uses it in his own speculative manner to indicate a concrete identity of opposites.)

Mathematics is a pure science, because the objectivity and regularity in quantitative relations which it studies, are at the same time grounded in and projected by the mathematical mind. Quantity, the ontological condition of all equations is also the condition of equated objects.

§200

Space is determined by *time* because every geometrical construction is possible only by moving points in temporal succession.

§201

Time, like space, is a pure form of the sensible or perceivable world (Anschauen usually translated as "intuition" simply means to perceive, too look at). Time is the condition of all perceiving immediate acts of experience *and* of that which is perceived and experienced. Nature is a spatial-temporal structure and process: If spatial structure is emphasized, the objectivity of nature is apparent; if time is emphasized, the subjectivity of nature is apparent. As perceived, nature is an endless and continuous *becoming*. Thus things are said to come and go *in* time. Things are not only in time: They are temporal; time is their very own mode of existence. Time is existential; it is the all-begetting, all-destroying Chronos. Every natural thing is temporal or transitory. This is the truth of nature. As true it is eternally true. The impossibility of natural things not to be temporal is their eternal necessity. Time is eternally what it is in each moment.

Eternity thus is not an abstraction, something that is supposed to be exempt from time; nor is it something before or after time—"before" and "after" are temporal dimensions. Rather, eternity is the absolute omnipresence of time, the absolute Now in all *times* (§42).

Time is negativity: The present moment is, but is vanishing; and vanished moments or moments to come *are* what they have been and what they will be.

This negativity of time, therefore, is an abstract and natural image or semblance of the subject. I distinguish in myself my own past, present, and future actions, and in all this I maintain my identity. Thus time is the external natural aspect in which the subject appears in its activity and freedom. I am, therefore, not only a temporal victim of time's power; I am also the power over it and responsible for my natural life-time (§53).

Reality in nature is thus both identical with and different from temporality. What was not there, comes to be there. What is there now comes not to be there later. Such is the nature of existential temporality or becoming spelled out in the temporal dimensions of past, present, and future—all held together in the unity of the eternal Now, in which beings and nonbeings eternally change into one another.

This concrete identity of eternal Now is not to be confused with the finite presence of an empirical natural duration. Finite durations in the present, future, or past may be abstractly isolated. They then lose their existential temporality and are transformed into object images; they are then more spatial than temporal and the targets of subjective memories, hopes, and fears.

If time is further "paralyzed," externalized, and quantified, we get time-units as equal and discreet moments in a continuum of movement. This is scientific clocktime, the basis of the arithmetical counting "one" and the many "ones." Arithmetic is thus, in analogy to geometry, the abstract science of time, and therefore applicable to physical movement which can be measured in arithmetical series.

Applied mathematics depends on stuff given in experience; it measures magnitudes and time relations of objects. Pure mathematics measures magnitudes and time relations in abstraction from empirical objects. Philosophy of applied and pure mathematics thinks space, time, and quantity as categories of nature as mathematical, and of mathematics as abstract natural science. Philosophy should not be confused with pure mathematics, and the latter should not be confused with empirical measure units. (This double confusion is widespread in philosophizing physicists of the 20th century.)

As distinct from pure and applied mathematical sciences, philosophy should neither imitate mathematical methods, as Spinoza has done, nor should it calculate and measure; but it may use mathematical terms symbolically. The Pythagoreans, for instance, have given famous examples of how one may use mathematical expressions as symbols of philosophical concepts. (A beautiful example of Hegel's use of a mathematical term as a philosophical symbol is found in §6.) Some expressions, for example "infinity," are used both in philosophy and mathematics. When this is done, however, the same terms convey different meanings. Philosophy comprehends mathematics dialectically as a synthesis a priori of space-time intuition and abstract reason.

§203

(In this § Hegel violates his own rule of §202 that philosophy should not interfere in scientific questions. His pseudo-dialectical "constructions" of "mass" and "matter" and physical "movement" as a transition to physics seem unintelligible to me. There is, however, the following important point:)

Matter does not *have* but *is* force or energy. Only because it acts and acts on others is it actual (wirklich). The expression (Aeusserung) of force is force itself, not an effect external to it. The externality of space-time relations in which this action and reaction or resistance takes place define forces as natural.

§204

The merit of Kant's *Metaphysical Principles of Natural Science* lies in its refutation of materialism and rationalism. He demonstrated that physical matter is not dead stuff having accidental secondary qualities and being governed by mechanical laws external to it. He developed the philosophical Concept of matter as a physical appearance and an equilibrium of living energies in tensions of attractions and repulsion. He has thus prompted a philosophy of nature which grasps its own organic Concept in the image of nature. He still, however, falsely assumed matter outside or prior to living energy (Hegel refers to page 119 of his *Logic I*, which corresponds in our text to §43, where he denies that there is a qualitative being behind or beyond all its own individually determined qualitative moments).

§205

General, particular, and *singular* aspects of the inorganic appearance of life corresponds to general, particular, and singular scientific descriptions of them.

§206

Matter, as appearing in masses or bodies, can be measured in quantitative units. How much or how many such aggregates are called wholes is superficial and arbitrary.

§207

The *inertia* of bodies seems to resist their dislocation and thus seems to resist the spatial-temporal process from which inert bodies nevertheless cannot escape.

§208

Physical *durations* are relative to one another; it is accidental (zufällig), which is considered to be at rest or in motion. This general relativity of rest and motion constitutes physical change, which is essential to all physical appearances.

Failing to grasp this dialectical concept, reason treats rest and motion as independent entities rather than as relative to one another.

§209

Spatial and temporal *locations* seem momentarily fixed; but such fixations do not last at all. (§202). All locations of all percepts are constantly changing in their relativity to one another.

§210

Gravitational systems require several bodies in constant tension of repulsion and attraction, and a continuous unity of relative motion and rest. Gravitation is resisted by inertia (§207), which concurrently contradicts the general physical relativity. Physical nature, therefore, is the concrete contradiction of resisting and not resisting its relativity (§208). This comprehensive identity of its many aspects is the living core of its appearing and existing moments (Dasein).

§211

The quantitative and mechanical relation of masses both abstracts from and is limited by their individual and qualitative relations.

§212

The physical world as absolute mechanism (§145) is at the same time the appearing image of absolute freedom, moving in and out of itself. Nature is not pushed around by something outside of it.

(Hegel praises Kepler for having seen the world as this living and moving image of eternity, or, in his own terminology, as a mirror of the absolute Idea. He pits Kepler's organic world-soul against Newton's mechanism of dead matter moved by mysterious forces external to it.)

PHYSICS

§213-217

(Hegel has stated the main idea of his philosophy of nature in §192-212. What follows in *physics* is mostly a dense fog of speculative fallacies and pseudo-dialectical contortions of physical problems. From the point of view of the philosophy, they are irrelevant; from the point of view of the sciences, they are unscientific interferences. I report a few passages, where Hegel finds natural-poetic symbols for his Concept.

Examples of particular problems of particular sciences irrelevant to philosophy: Pressure (§213), fall (§214), pendulum (§215), center of gravity (§216).

Examples of pseudo-dialectical contortions: "But the necessity of the concept appears in this sphere of externality as an external obstacle or as *friction*"

174

(§215); or "the distinction of central bodies from dependent ones is not the in-it-selfness of gravity whose identical nature is their existence" (§216).

§218

Nature as a system of active elements in dynamic relations is the appearing image of the ontological essence of being: Nature is essentially dialectical in its qualitative polarities.

§219-220

Light is both focused in celestial and in the early centers, but it is also an omnipresent diffusion.

It is a condition of individuated life, of seeing, and of being seen.

It is a natural symbol of truth and goodness, and for this reason rightly worshipped in natural religions.

Newton's mechanical analysis of light as consisting of corpuscles or waves and his equally mechanical compositions of light as a result of rotating dark colors leaves the original concrete phenomenon of light out of sight, and leaves sight out of comprehension.

§221

Light is nothing apart from its dialectical opposite: Darkness; light is the not-dark, as dark is the not-light.

This concrete qualitative interpenetration of light and darkness appears in the realm of real *colors*.

Goethe's theory of colors truly studies them in their qualitative concreteness and in their qualitative orders ("colors are the deeds and passions of life." Goethe)

Newton falsely claims that light is composed of five or seven dark colors; and he confuses general mathematical-mechanical theories about light and color with light and color themselves.

§222-224

(Out of a chaos of pseudo-dialectical fallacies emerge here and there astronomical morsels like stars, suns, planets, the moon, meteorites, comets.) From §224: Kepler's profound faith to comprehend the planets according to the proportions of a celestial musical harmony should not be despised as a mere aberration of fancy, but esteemed as an expression of comprehensiveness.

Astronomy, however, cannot discover a real law, let alone such harmonious comprehensiveness, either in the distribution of or in the distance of planets.

(Hegel then alludes to his Jena disertation, entitled: De orbitis planetarum, and confesses that his youthful attempt to follow hypothetically Kepler's dreams of a cosmic harmony can no longer be considered as satisfactory.)

§225-233

(Here Hegel poetically describes aesthetic qualities of nature which were called the four elements in early Greek cosmology: Earth, water, air, fire.) *Air* is an all-pervasive, transparent life-sustaining fluidity; an unsuspected (verdachtlos) but nevertheless also a sneaking life-consuming or corroding power in all mechanical and individual processes.

Fire is a material symbol of all-devouring time. Fanned by air, it exists in destroying the conditions of its own existence. It destroys its own destructiveness.

As warmth in the organism it is the flickering unrest of life, a constant conflagration.

Water is the quiet possibility of dissolution; it is the opposite to the disquiet process of fire. Like air, it is shapeless, but unlike air it forms shaped bodies conditioned and surrounded by solid earth.

Earth is the individual totality of all elements and elementary processes.

§230-259

(In a wasteland of pseudo-dialectical fallacies, Hegel "construes": Metereology [§230], crystals [§231], thunderstorms [§232], "the earth is first the *abstract* ground of individuality positing itself in its negative unity of all abstract elements which run away from each other" [§233], shape [§234], composites [§235], density [§236], brittleness [§237], globe [§239], cohesion [§240], adhesion [§241], elasticity [§242], sound as "specified reality" [§243], "cancellation (aufheben) of cohesion is warmth-capacity" [§244].)

§232-238

(Here Hegel succeeds in finding a natural symbol, an external image of his concrete dialectical unity of opposites.)

Magnetism is one of the most immanent natural determinations in which philosophy of nature could meet and find its own concrete thought in a natural shape and image. The magnet represents in a simple naive fashion the nature of the Concept. Its poles are not material things—they have not a sensuous mechanical reality—but they are ideal moments within their dynamic unity. Positive and negative poles both attract and repel one another. The indifference and identity of magnetism differentiates itself; the differentiated poles together enact their unity apart from which they are nothing.

The South-North orientation of magnetic needles points to the magnetism of the earth.

177

§245

Every individual body of nature is a totality of elementary processes and is in turn qualifying them; they enter the organic process of the individual body, and are also related to unbound elements outside the individual natural body.

The concreteness and complexity of these relations resembles comprehensiveness which does not merely abstract or isolate them but thinks them together and is undeterred by the muddled confusion and perfunctory experience which the sensuous appearance presents.

Comprehension admires the violence of reason by which it tore general elements out of sensuous things and identified them in general terms. Although reason does not reach concrete comprehension, it nevertheless is elevated above a thoughtless and chaotic empirical tale of haphazard events.

§246-248

The senses in organisms are correlative to various elements. Through them the organism is in contact with the elementary life; but they also are restrictions, protecting the organisms against it. In their intercourse with one another, individual bodies rise above mechanical behavior patterns. They respond to each other, for example, by producing sounds through their own vibrations.

§250

(A typical pseudo-dialectical "transition" to chemistry: "The *whole corporeity* thus is involved in the tension and in the process which is the *formation* and singularization of an individual body: The *chemical process*"!)

CHEMISTRY

§251-259

(Various chemical objects are picked up at random and are pseudo-dialectically "construed." After Hegel has succeeded in making them perfectly ununderstandable, he blames the "impotence of nature" [§253] not to be able to follow his speculative fallacies: Metallity [§251], water—"the element *water* is the middle, whereby the *concept* of genuine differences, which is the *unity* of both and the *essence* of each in itself, joins itself with its *reality*—or which identifies the difference of each with the difference of the other, and thereby becomes *real* as totality of its concept and is, against the immediate solidity of extremes, *abstract* neutrality"—now we know what the "element" H_2O *really* is! [§252]: Oxygen and hydrogen [§253] sulfur, nitrogen [§254] carbon [§255] acids, alkalines, salt [§256].)

§257-259 (§335-336)

The life of nature culminates in the chemical process; it is the analogy or semblance (Anschein) of life. If the chemical products could renew their activity or procreate themselves, they would be alive. Life is a chemical process perennially restoring itself. Individual bodies are produced in and by their chemical processes, but chemical processes are also their destruction. Producing and destroying individuals is the natural life as a qualitative process underlying its chemical appearance.

Taken in abstraction from its living actuality, the chemical process is and expresses the infinite relativity and futility of all natural things. All appear in qualities, pass over into one another and continually change each other in an infinite number of respects. Any individual shape is inexhaustable and a complete description of it is impossible; it would consist of all changes and cycles of changes which it goes through and reflects during its whole existence. And no such existence can hold out, it never can stay in any final shape. The sum total of actions and reaction appearing in the infinite qualitative changes of all things rushes forward on the road to its own death, like fire in consuming other energies consumes itself.

The absolute form of nature is its unrest, agitation, movement; its dialectic is recognized in the chemical process in which all qualities of mortal bodies are drawn into this relativity and transitoriness. The chemical process is the highest manifestation of the appearing life of inorganic nature; here we grasp its objective time, the unperishable fire of life, as Heraclitus puts it.

As soon as life relates itself to its own unity, it shows itself to be the organizing immaterial soul appearing in material embodiments. The qualitative process thus becomes for itself what it is in itself: The infinite form of immaterial individuality.

But this natural soul remains tied to its appearance and does not reach its objectivity in thought and spiritual spontaneity, which could kindle and fan and determine itself. Mechanism was cancelled, reserved, and elevated (aufgehoben) in chemism; and chemism was *aufgehoben* in organic life—in this philosophical reflection, nature herself in us and through us has "reflected" itself into itself and reached its own actuality, which is life. Nature is thus beginning to overcome its superficiality and externality and assembles its life in non-sensuous centers of activity or subjects. We thus move from the prose to the poesy of nature ("poesy derived from Greek poieisis": Creative activity).

THE EARTH

§260

The Idea—the final cause and teleological process of the whole (§187-191)—gains existence in the life of nature but is also estranged from itself.

The earth as a geological totality is an organism, individual shape and image of cosmic life; in the levels of vegetative life, the earth is alive in itself and in animal life it is, furthermore, alive for itself.

§261

The earth is a living whole or an individual organism because it is the totality of all of its own chemical processes, which it perennially keeps going on; it is not consumed by them as natural things are, but maintains itself through them as their organizing unity. The earth is both immediate subject of all its activities as well as its own object-product. In its visible shape the earth is also the embodiment of its cosmic past and of cosmic powers beyond it.

§262-263

The distribution of continents and oceans, of geological structures and atmospheric, meterological conditions are both immediate and mediated as results of the history of the earth.

This individual history of the earth's organism is also linked to the historical becoming of the solar system: In its movement and relative position to other planets, to the moon and comets; in the inclination of its axis, and in its magnetic axis.

The geological layers and strata of rock-formation and erosions and deposits, the formation of metals and minerals form an ascending scale of levels (Stufengang) from inorganic organizations towards organic organizations, counteracted by shapeless deteriorations.

§265 (§343)

What the earth is in itself—a total individual organic whole of life, an objective subject, qualitatively completely determined—becomes for itself what it is in itself: Fertile earth blossoms out in actual active organisms, mechanical and elementary processes are transformed and individualized in plants and animals.

THE PLANT

§266 (§344)

Every plant is a unique individual like Mother Earth is. The plant treats the earth as a means of subsistence, as soil, which is used by the plant. It transforms the elementary life of nature—earth, water, warmth, air—into its own organic life.

Geometrical reason, which made itself visible in the crystal, becomes more flexible in the plant which makes use of linear construction in its stems and veins; of planes in its leaves, greatly varied in its incisions, in its rounded or pointed edges; and of the sphere in its seeds and fruits.

The polarity of magnetic and electric nature and of light and darkness is taken up into the vegetative soul of the plants. They stretch themselves towards the light and sink into the dark soil; and create their own color in the flower.

The general kind of a plant is immediately identical with every one of its individual shapes and is constantly reproducing itself through infinite individual variations; while the individual plants, on the other hand, serve the general plan of its organization, while it seems to exist only for itself.

This immediate unity of general and individual processes of assimilation, growth, and reproduction of kinds makes mobility unnecessary.

The unity of vegetative societies maintains itself in the infinite multiplication of differentiation of its kinds and individuals; it not only reproduces but also feeds itself by making its own humus.

The processes of its quantitative growth and its qualitative metabolism of elements are at the same time the processes of its decay; cells, fibers, and the like multiply until they smother the plant in dead wood (Verholzung).

The lower the vegetable organism is, the less differentiated are its parts; every part can become the whole organism.

In the more differentiated and higher formation: Root, stem, leaf, and blossom are still differentiations of a fluid whole and each in turn may become a whole plant again or exchange functions—as when branches planted in the earth turn into roots and the former roots turn into branches.

Goethe's *Metamorphosis of Plants* began this comprehensive thought on the nature of the plant; he overcame the external classification of abstract particularities and drew them into the comprehension of the unity of life. The identity of all organs in the metamorphosis of plants is the Concept of their fluid self-differentiation.

(Hegel describes four processes which in their interaction, together constitute the organic Concept of plant life; shaping process, growing and decaying process in the formation of organs, metabolism of elements, propagating process through flowers and seeds.

In the fourth edition of the *Encyclopedia*, the editor Michelet stuffed these few paragraphs with lecture notes so that they degenerate into an eighty-page course in botany. I report from its §364.)

The seed is potentially or ideally a whole plant, an immediate unity of a unique individual and its general type. The earth is the general possibility of this organic potentiality to actualize itself and to embody its living power (Kraft).

To plant the seed into the earth is therefore a mystic, magic action. It depends on and trusts the mysterious power which is slumbering in the seed. It indicates that there is more to it than appears in its immediacy; planting the seed is a natural analogy of baptism where the helpless infant is solemnly received as a member of a spiritual realm—the magician which helps the seed to gain a new value—like Aladdin rubbing the rusty lamp—is the Concept of nature. The seed is the power which conjures the earth, that its living energies may serve its life.

§271-272 (§349)

Vegetative life—as a circular and individuated process moving, modifying, and reproducing itself —is a natural analogy of the Concept or subject; it is the Concept externalized in space-time locations.

The plant—although imaginatively shaping, nourishing, and propagating itself—never comes to itself, but always goes out and falls apart in new individuals. It does not exist for itself—it has no self—it exists for others. The splendor of its aroma and of its colors is there to be seen, smelled, and tasted by others. The life of the plant, thus, is a life of selfless sacrifice, poetically called the innocence of the plant. The animal organism is reached as soon as this vegetative life turns inward and becomes life for itself. In its higher forms, animal individuals are alive not only for themselves but also for each other.

THE ANIMAL

§273-298

(The weakness of Hegel's philosophy of nature is just as prevalent in this section as it was in the last. On the one hand, he picks up elementary zoological concepts which have no philosophical significance; on the other hand, he "construes" them in pseudo-dialectical verbiage which is as unscientific as it is un-philosophical; and to add insult to injury, he constantly quarrels with the ordinary scientific method to which he owes all his facts: Classifications of animals into vertebrates and non-vertebrates, or of animals with warm red blood and animals without; classifications of physiological systems of sensitivity, irritability, and reproduction; facts from comparative anatomy, or bone structures, or physiological functions of nerves, muscles, blood, bowels, plants, cells, etc.

There is, nevertheless, a thin thread running through this chaotic maze in which his original philosophy of nature—the idea in its self-estrangement—is further pursued.)

The plant is interwoven with its environment, whereas the animal breaks this immediate context. It is alive for itself. The animal soul is the inner unity of the whole animal, wholly present in all its functions. Corresponding to this concentration in itself, the environment becomes for the animal an outer world, to which it has to adapt itself. Whereas in the plants the elementary life of nature in earth, water, air, and light is directly absorbed; the animal, on the contrary, transforms the elementary life of organic and inorganic nature into stimuli to which it responds in many ingenious ways.

Fish learn to swim, breathe, and see in water; birds and insects take to the air on wings; reptiles and mammals learn to live with the earth.

In each realm of animal life there are levels of lower and higher organization which are higher or lower in regard to their more simple or more complex forms of organization.

The sexual differentiation of animals gives rise to animal families or animal societies. The sexual copulation fuses independent individuals which are in need of and dependent upon each other. In the act of copulation, the animal actualizes the concreteness of their kind which is reproducing itself through them. (The German word Gattung means kind, genus, race; the word Begattung means copulation, pairing. To Hegel this is a welcome linguistic help to express his concrete universal: Begattung integrating individuals actualizes their Gattung in a stream of generations of rising and vanishing individuals.)

The longing to be one with another and the feeling of this achieved union with its partner is the highest pleasure of animal life. Lower forms exist only to reproduce themselves; their act of copulation is also their death.

The separation and opposition of an inward animal soul against its external environment is identical with animal *mobility:* In order to seek food and to adapt itself, the animal explores its life-space and shapes itself according to its ends.

This selfish purposiveness determines the visible shape of the animal organism: Claws and sharp teeth express the purpose of animals of prey, hoofs and broad teeth express the purpose of feeding on plants.

This inner organic purposiveness in action and process is the Idea insofar as it gains existence in animal life; but as natural and external, the Idea is also frustrated and alienated from itself. It tends to develop beautiful types and individuals, representting their types; but it also fails and develops monstrosities: If fish take to swamp, crawl on land and come amphibious; or if a bird, like the ostrich, tramples camel-like through deserts with ridiculous rudiments of wings and feathers that are like rough fur; or if mice sprout wings and zig-zag as bats through the twilight; or if a mammal, the duckbill imitates a duck and helps himself to a beak; or if it is not even clear whether an organism is a plant or an animal—then the types are mixed up and confusion reigns. It is as if a musician wanted to paint with tones, or as if an historian would dramatize his dry stories in blank verse. The second frustration of the Idea is the sadness and brutality of animal life. The purpose of every animal is to maintain itself; violently driven by instinct and greed, ruthlessly at the expense of others. Violent death is the general fate of animals. Each animal has to fight with all it is and has for its survival. Anxiety and alarm are the most common feeling; they express themselves in protective organs of escape, mimicry, and simulation. At the mercy of external circumstances, victim of luck and chance, the animal is threatened from all sides and is suffering fear, pain, and sickness.

The glory of organic teleology is amply balanced by the misery of mutual self-estrangement. This inadequacy of the natural appearance of the Idea, this self-estrangement is a sickness unto death, for which there is no remedy in nature. Animal life is insecure, dreadful, brutal; left to itself it is the complete futility of finite and external existence.

PHILOSOPHY OF THE SPIRIT

(In the second edition of the *Encyclopedia* Hegel inserted an *Introduction* to the philosophy of the spirit. I follow it from §377-386, replacing the corresponding sketch of the first edition in §299-306.)

§377

Know thyself is an absolute imperative to fulfill. It is the most concrete, the highest, and most difficult task which mind can set for itself.

Self-knowledge of the spirit intends to know its true essence; truth as it actually exists in and for itself. This spiritual truth becomes the objective content and value of the human soul.

This Mind or Spirit (Geist) is the concrete universal and substantial core of human existence. It is presupposed and blindly taken for granted by empirical psychology, which is mainly engaged in the study of individual weaknesses, inclinations, peculiarities, passions and aberrations—the so-called folds of the heart.

§378

Mind-spirit (Geist) unites its own essential unity with its equally essential many partial and individual manifestations.

Philosophy as self-knowledge must therefore heal the split between a non-appearing soul as rationalistic metaphysics had it (§23) and a mass of empirical details without spiritual orientation.

191

Aristotle's work on the soul—the soul is immanent purposiveness (entelechy) giving directions to its organic life and visible embodiments—is still the most excellent, even unique treatise of this problem. The essential purpose of the philosophy of the spirit must re-introduce dialectical concreteness into spiritual self-knowledge; this would again disclose the profound meaning of Aristotle's works.

§379

The living unity of the spirit is an immediate *feeling* which the self has of itself (Selbstgefühl). This feeling is diametrically opposed to representational thinking in object-images, which falsifies the felt unity of life by cutting it up into various disconnected faculties.

The spirit in its psycho-physical embodiments is both free and determined. These opposites are immediately felt as one, as a dialectical unity which can be comprehended but not rationally thought (§86-87).

Phenomena of "animal magnetism," what is now called psychical research, has shown the substantial unity of the soul and its power to be in immediate communication with other souls. This ideality of pervasive feeling confuses reason, which cannot handle it with its abstract separations, but is quite in line with the speculative need to overcome rationalistic prejudices.

§380

Implicit in its concrete nature is a difficulty peculiar to the contemplation of the spirit. The many levels within its development are stations in its own maturing of self-realization; they are retained, as lower levels functioning together with higher levels. This differentiates the soul from nature where earlier strata of its life are left behind and are visible in their externality: The general mechanism of mass-movements disregarding its qualitative individuation are conditions of the solar systems; it in turn is the condition of organizing elementary life in the earth; and the earth is the condition of organic life, with its sensibilities and sense-qualities corresponding to its sensibility.

As distinct from nature, spirit retains in its development its earlier levels and phases as essential moments, moods, mental states and determinations; at the same time, its lower and earlier functions anticipate and foreshadow higher potentialities. Sleep, for example, is potential awakening in which it is known as sleep. The higher functions are rooted in simple sentient experience, which in turn is seen as bare abstract beginning from the point of view of later and developed contents.

§381

Concept—the identity of subject-object—exists in nature in external objectivity. When this self-alienation is broken through, Concept gains a subjective objectivity for itself. Nature then actualizes its potential truth in the self of the spirit. In turn, spirit recognizes in nature its own presupposition and finds its own dialectic reflected in its own analogies of itself. Concept thus wrests from nature its true identity with itself. The primacy of the spirit over nature —which precedes it in time—lies in this absolute negativity which overcomes its natural externality, transforming it into means of expression of itself. Only in this work can spirit overcome its immediacy and gain its subjective identity for itself. But further than that, it does not only make nature its object, it makes itself its own object; this subject-object is its own product wherein the Idea is actualized and becomes real for itself.

The identity of the spirit is also its own non-identity with anything given. This absolute negativity is its own freedom; it is the essence of the spirit (§40).

Spirit is, therefore, that which is able to abstract itself not only from all external conditions but also from its own previous embodiments (§42). It can endure and suffer the negation of its individual immediacy and nevertheless affirm its freedom and its identity with itself in all such painful negations. In consciousness the negativity of the finite is sorrow (Schmerz). It is through this sacrificial work and suffering that the spirit affirms its true infinity (§48).

This spiritual universality is also its omnipresence in all members of the spiritual community (§43). Spirit is the subject making itself its own object and thus is in and for itself. In this activity it reveals itself, shows forth what it is, what it has been, and what it can be. In the spirit, possibility and actuality (Wirklichkeit) coincide.

What spirit is, does, and can be when it produces itself is not an entity or "thing" (Etwas, §44-46). The spirit is its own product which is not external to or distinguishable from its activity as form and content are distinguishable in things. Forms and contents of the spirit both are its self-determination and are nothing apart from self-revelation.

Man as spirit presupposes nature as an independent objective world, but at the same time posits it as possibility for his own freedom. Spirit, further, finds its own Concept evidently reflected in nature and in the speculative sense transforms it into the image of its own free being. Spirit thus reveals the world and recreates it in and as its own being. Spirit affirms and gives to itself the certainty and truth of its freedom. The dialectic of Being prepared the truth of spirit and its freedom. The transition of the Origin into that which begins in it, is in the abstract logic of Being the ontological analogy of the self-revelation of spirit (§41-42).

The Absolute is Spirit—this is its ultimate definition.

To find this definition and to comprehend its meaning and content is the absolute tendency motivating all true cultures and their philosophy. All religion and Science are concentrated on this point. This absolute tendency alone makes the history of the world comprehensible.

Words and representational images of the absolute spirit are found in early thought; the message of the Christian religion is to reveal God as spirit: God is a spirit and those who worship him should worship him in spirit and in truth (Hegel's favorite passage from the New Testament).

Philosophy must comprehend in its own medium the essential truth given in mythical object-imagery. This task cannot be fulfilled and the problem cannot be adequately solved unless philosophy moves in the element of the Concept which is its necessary form. These two sides, the absolute freedom of the spirit and the necessity of its form, are its objective content and its soul.

§385

Spirit is self-development: As *subjective spirit* or *natural soul* it tends towards realizing its Concept. The soul realizes itself as a being which is in and for itself, which relates itself to itself. In overcoming its immediacy, it reaches out towards freedom and agreement with itself.

As *objective spirit* or *mind*, spirit finds its freedom in an objective and necessary moral world-order, which it has produced and in which it takes part. Its aim is to find itself in this order of a reality with which it is confronted (vorhanden).

The absolute spirit finds itself united with truth. It realizes its identity with all being which is both an objective subjectivity and a subjective objectivity. The absolute spirit is actualized in art, religion, and philosophy.

§386

Philosophy of Spirit is divided into two major parts. The first—subjective spirit or soul and objective spirit or mind—deals with the finite in the infinite; the second—absolute spirit—with the infinite in the finite spirit.

Finite spirit rises through many levels of its activity until it reaches its true identity in the light of which its previous phases and ascending steps are known in their truth. Concurrently each finite station and level in this ascent of the spirit is an obstacle and dim light (Schein) which the spirit has created in and for itself, in order to pass beyond it, in its very retention of it.

In breaking through its own self-producing limitations and in appreciating and preserving them as such in its absolute totality, spirit liberates itself from them and thus reaches its Concept. This is its freedom.

As one and the same, spirit finds a given world and engenders itself in appropriating it, and emancipates itself in its finitude from its finitude. The unity of infinite and finite spirit, wherein each is both caught up and free in the other, is absolute spirit.

The greatest and toughest of all obstacles is the standpoint of *reason*. Clinging to the finite as if it were ultimate and to abstract fixations as if they were absolute, in its false modesty, reason thus tries to ward off the comprehensiveness of the spirit. In its extreme form, this stubborn insistence on metaphysical untruth is *evil*. Absolute spirit, however, eternal in and for itself, annihilates this annihilation of finite reason and makes vain this vanity.

THE NATURAL SOUL

§307

The natural soul in its immediacy is immersed in the unconscious life of nature. In breaking this immediacy, it distinguishes itself from a self-opposed, a natural, living environment. This is the beginning and an analogy of what later will turn out to be a comprehensive subject-object, wherein the subject makes itself its own object or problem, and develops objectivity within itself.

The soul awakens to consciousness, consciousness awakens to self-consciousness, and self-consciousness becomes comprehensive when it participates in and unites itself to the world. Potentially the soul is this budding comprehension. Its ascent and development is thus to actualize for itself what it potentially is in itself. "One may just as well say: The soul is first merely objective and should become truly subjective; as to say the soul is first merely subjective and should become truly objective. On the one hand, objective contents are subjectively appropriated— empty abstract subjectivity is filled; on the other hand, general objective contents find their living organs, their conscious representatives." (X, 48)

§308

In the soul, nature herself begins to overcome its externality in assembling and collecting natural instincts, appetites, functions in an indivisible, individual unity. In distinction from the unconscious elementary and organic-vegetative life, the natural soul is awake.

§309 (§389)

But as not yet conscious of itself, as self-conscious I am or spirit, the natural soul is still subconscious or asleep. The waking life of nature is the slumber of the spirit.

Lacking heaviness and all other sensuous qualities, the soul is non-physical or immaterial. As diffused throughout nature, it is the world-soul.

Even the highest spheres of particular activity and the most outstanding manifestations of spirit could not exist without this all-pervasive presence of this living substance or world-soul which remains their absolute pre-condition. Life is potentiality, lending itself to and in turn being shaped by all higher formations of life.

Physical qualities, perceived by the sensing functions of the soul, are in reality qualities of life. In appearance, wherein all life is individuated, they are objectified. In its physical appearance life is given to all individuals in the form of self-estrangement. Physical "matter," however, is not real in and for itself—it may be treated as if it could be observed in pure externality and in abstraction from cosmic life.

Even to the physicist of recent times, matter has become thinner and imponderable.

Reason has transformed the dialectical unity of the psycho-physical polarity into an abstract dualism of two independent entities: extended body and unextended soul. From this perspective the concrete dialectical interrelation between body and soul becomes a completely incomprehensible mystery. (A full treatment of this psycho-physical dialectic is found in my chapter on *Soul and Body* in *Dialectic. A way into and within philosophy*. New York. Bookman Associates. 1953.)

"Descartes, Malebranche, Spinoza, Leibnitz all sought the solution of the psycho-physical riddle in God, who thus became the asylum of ignorance. If God alone is the unity of soul and body, both lose their own dialectical existence and reality and disappear in him.

"Leibnitz came closest to the solution. His monads are creative centers of life which, as external to each other, appear as phenomena and physical aggregates; he failed, however, to see that monads are not absolutely separated, but are actual individual modifications of one and the same life. To insist on this unity is the merit of Spinoza."

"Materialism is self-refuting. Its proposition: 'All is matter' is in no sense matter, but a proposition presupposing the thinking mind in whom and for whom alone propositions are true or false. Compared with an abstract rationalistic dualism, however, materialism is to be recommended for its enthusiasm in a unitary world (X 60)."

"Pantheism or panpsychism is an enthusiastic feeling for the unity of life in all Beings. It is akin to a youthful view wherein we feel ourselves in brotherly sympathy with the whole of nature and all fellow creatures; life appeals to us and envelops us on all sides. We feel the immaterial world-soul in unison with a felt and given nature.

"But pantheism is only a reveling life, a bacchanalian intuition, and does not proceed to clear distinctions and articulations of the problem. The distinct and concrete shapes are not respected in their differences but dissolved in a sublime and immense infinity of feeling. We cannot remain in the immediacy of an enthusiastic feeling, but must proceed to systematic thought, which will also explain appearances in their external objectivity (X, 55f)."

The world-soul must not be isolated and fixed in abstraction; there is no life-in-general apart from its actual individuations (§43).

§310

The soul is not conscious of its organic embodiment (Leiblichkeit), which is identical with its unconsciousness, submerged and immersed in its natural substance, the world-soul.

§311 (§392)

Through this, its organic embodiment, the soul participates in the planetary life of the earth; moods are in tune with changes in climates, seasons, and hours of the day. While animals live essentially in a sympathetic rapport with nature, in cultured man this rapport is subordinate. If it is given importance and if the natural soul begins to dominate the self-conscious soul, this domination of natural moods results in depressions and, in extreme cases, insanity. Primitive man, like animals, who lives in immediate contact with the cosmic world-soul, specifically with the life of the earth—self-conscious soul being undeveloped—has powers of presentiments of situations and events and a feeling for suggestions, which to civilized man seem miraculous.

§312 (§393)

Geographical formations and structures of the earth—such as the distribution of seas and mountains —are reflected in the differentiation of natural races of animals and humans, and in their adaptations to their environment. The same environment may stimulate quite different responses. There is no one-way causality, but inter-activity (§104).

§313 (§394)

Such general conditions and differentiations of life are *particularized* in national and local mores, occupations, bodily shapes, dispositions and skills; and further, in the inner tendencies and abilities of the intelligence and morality of peoples and groups.

The history of peoples shows the duration of such national types throughout all periods back to their first appearance.

§314

"Just as Being originates itself in its omnipresence and determines itself in its qualitative uniqueness, so the soul also actualizes itself in its own individual modifications" (X. 61).

The Concept of the soul is the unity of its general, particular, and individual subjectivity. In every individual, the Concept is modified; it appears in the infinite variability of temperaments, artistic genius, natural talents, characters, physiognomies and idiosyncrasies of families and singular individuals.

§315

The immediate original division (Ur-teil!) of the natural soul is its rhythm of being asleep and of being awake. Alternative opposites of sleeping and waking are equally necessary conditions for the preservation of the natural soul.

§316

The soul, in becoming aware of itself as alive and awake, distinguishes itself from its own indistinct subconscious substance as *this* individual unit of life.

The initial act of awakening is the condition of all activities of mind and spirit. Sleep is not only a rest or a relaxation from daily activities, but it is also a return from the workaday world of dispersion and details to the substantial power and reservoir of such activity.

As the individual wrests himself away from his unconscious background of cosmic life, he hands himself over to the natural course of changes which belong to being awake and being an individual for himself. The whole course of his growth and decay is determined by the ages of life in their natural sequence:

"*Birth* is the enormous qualitative leap from subconscious nature into potential human existence (X. 98).

In the *infant*, spirit is still wrapped up or enveloped in its potentiality; it is potentially human.

Childhood is the age of natural harmony and satisfaction with himself and with his environment. The child thrives on the feeling of love for its parents, and in the feeling to be loved by them.

The *youth* develops tensions: Subjective ideals, illusions of grandeur, ambitions to live up to worshipped heroes, the question of what he ought to become, are all in tension and conflict with his immediate singularity. He feels the conflict between an objective world and his unreadiness and immaturity for it. The dreams, which he has idealized, clash with the repeated experience of non-fulfillment. And this shock, in turn, drives him to seek compensation in his ideal dreams.

The mature *man* acknowledges the necessity and comprehensiveness of an objective moral world-order into which he has entered and taken his place. In his activity he participates in a common work and in a growing concern for inter-activities which he enriches and by which his worth is proved and approved. Actual presence and objective value fuse. He has made himself to be what he is in co-operation with others.

The *old man* gains the freedom from restricting interests and worries; he is above the turmoil of his present time, which has become external to him. His unity with the objective world-order is a contemplative accomplishment.

As *senile* his activity is shrinking; nature reduces him to passive habits and dull routines—the beginning of death.

In *death* natural life is victorious and cancels its own individual modification." (X. 95)

"This physiological evolution from cradle to grave (Entwicklung) should not be confused with the unfolding (Entfaltung) of spirit." (X. 96)

§318

The soul is alive for itself; it is at once a closed system of its inner functions and open towards the outside: It at once feels itself in feeling the other. Its sensing, perceiving functions are interfused with what is sensed and perceived; and sensed qualities are immediately fused with feeling tones, such as agreeable or disagreeable. The inner sense is a sympathetic identification (Mitleben) of the soul with all its functions, appetites, and desires. Courage and wrath, thinking and professional occupations are immediately felt functions of the self. When they are looked at from the outside, they are located in the reproductive and sensitive systems of the organism—in the intestine, the breast, and the head.

§319 (§403)

The soul is in tension: On the one hand, it is a subjective center for itself and, on the other hand, it remains tied to a vast subconscious substantial life. I am a simple, bottomless pit sunk into an infinite abundance of possible or virtual experiences. The individual never knows how many experiences have been experienced and absorbed by him or how many he has forgotten. In abnormal states memories of things forgotten are sometimes brought back. As a unique subjective center of all its functions, the soul is a monad: It carves out of its experience the totality of a particular world-view in which it mirrors itself. As a living mirror of the universe, it is the actual and individual existence of the speculative Concept.

§320 (§405)

The natural subconscious life may prevail in the soul, as the mother prevails in the embryo. Dreams, prophecies, presentiments, telepathy, clairvoyance, somnambulism, hypnosis, and unconscious suggestions immediately felt—all those so-called occult facts are evidence for the immediate immersion of the soul in non-spatial, purely functional relationships with natural life.

The danger of those archaic functions is that they may erupt in physical disturbance or mental sickness in a conscious cultured person. At best, the magic circle of obsessions and enchantments minimizes and reduces a free self-conscious personality.

In any event, it is a confusion of categories to expect valuable knowledge to be gained from trances and spiritualistic seances.

§321 (§408)

The conscious soul may lose control over its irrational, subconscious dream-life; the latter intruding into waking life. This loss of unity or split of the soul, and the perversion of its order, is *insanity*, of all kinds and degrees. Such misfortune (Unglück), in its most virulent form, is evil: Insanity, triumphant in waking life as a tyrannical power, is the evil demon of man.

It is often difficult to determine whether or not an ordinary passion, illusion, or error is the beginning of insanity.

In the thoughtful, benevolent, humane treatment of mental patients, one should keep in mind the Socratic principle of ethics. Every evil is a mistaken and misplaced good wherein the concrete unity of the soul is only disturbed, but not entirely lost or depraved. The latter, the completely irredeemable loss of unity, would be *suicide*.

§322

The soul—in order to become what it ought to be—must fight its immediacy, while also preserving it as subordinate potential for its conscious purposiveness. In working at itself, it proves its power of controlling (übergreifend), making use of its irrational immediacy.

§323

This must not be misunderstood as if the soul should be hostile towards its organic life. This would be insanity in reverse: If the spirit fights against its natural organic existence, it remains negatively fascinated by it. Such a negative abstraction leads one to mistreat life as if it were an external object, blind fate, an overwhelming evil to be eradicated. Such a false spiritualism or *moralism* also is loss of concrete unity.

§324

The true relation of the conscious and the unconscious self, then, is this: The soul preserves its unity in meeting itself in all of its subconscious functions. As concrete identity it is present for itself in its living organization (Leib). In waking up, it breaks through its immediacy; concurrently it preserves and uses its immediacy to serve purposes going beyond the immediate living. The organism thus belongs to the soul, as a musical instrument belongs to the artist, or as a predicate belongs to the logical subject of which it is a true expression.

§325 (§410)

The soul is working on itself and thus exists as an educational process. It gladly gets hold of and penetrates its natural powers; repetition of actions serving purposes brings about and establishes habits; habits accumulate in skills. The soul thus prepares itself and makes itself fit for its activity in the world. It retains acquired habits and skills as a second nature, having made them inward, remembered (erinnert) possessions with which it maintains its identity. It can give account of them and is accountable for them. The subject has produced its own second nature; at the same time the product of his own subjective activity is a self-created objective state of affairs.

The consciously, as well as unconsciously, produced subject-object is the beginning of freedom, wherein the soul is one and in agreement with itself; freedom is the supreme end. Habits that do not contribute towards this end but enslave the soul are *bad habits;* if they accumulate into dull repetitious patterns, they lead to death and are the beginning of death in life.

§326 (§411)

Language transfigures physical sounds into *signs* through which the soul communicates its presence and actuality to others. The same holds true for preverbal communication: Gestures and movements of the living body (Leib), laughing and weeping, the tone in which something is said, the physiognomic figures and body-types—are all instrumental signs which in turn are interpreted as expressions of the

soul by others. Its actuality lies in the mutual interpretation and in the identity of its inner life with its
voluntary or involuntary signs.

In the interpretation of signs, however, the differences between inner and outer must not be overlooked; for the dialectical identity of opposites, which
is not immediate, must be remembered. Taken in its
immediacy, appearance is always contingent and uncertain. Physiognomy, for example, is not an immediate knowledge of the soul, whose freedom transcends its momentary expressions; it may even use
them to hide itself from the interpreter.

§327 (§412)

In consciously treating the physical as a sign of
its freedom, the soul becomes *subjective spirit* and
mind, the conscious "I am." Subjective thinking acts
upon, opposes and relates itself to an external world
which is transformed into an object of its thought
and action. This conscious subjective spirit is a second
and higher awakening of the soul; it now lives in a
conscious subject-object relation to itself as well as
to others.

SUBJECTIVE MIND

(Hegel changed the title *Phaenomenologie des
Geistes* of the first edition—to *Subjektiver Geist* in the
second edition. It is, indeed, a summary of his first
part of the *Phenomenology of Mind* of 1806. In this
section I am rendering *Geist* as mind.)

§329 (§413)

The subjective mind appears in every individual
consciousness. "It begins to *struggle* with external objects, which struggle is a higher value than the naive
unity of the natural soul with its subconscious cosmic

life." (X. 258) The subjective mind is simultaneously aware and certain of its conscious self as well as of its natural soul which it now opposes to itself as its own object and material to be shaped. The "I am," thus, is one side of this relation and at the same time the whole relation; in being aware of myself as my own object I am self-reflection. In the world of nature *light* is an analogy to this: By manifesting itself it makes a visible world evident to sight.

§330 (§414)

And as light reveals darkness, so natural existence becomes for mind a dark region below its consciousness; this dialectic of light and dark, high and low, is absent in the animal soul.

§331-332

There is a further conflict between subjective mind as a conscious being-for-itself and the object which it poses and presupposes as an alien, given thing.

In *Fichte* this is the perennial problem of how I should handle the Not-I. For him there is no dialectical unity with both as poles of the same process. They only *ought* to be united—which ought prevents them from ever being united. Fichte's error lies in the false initial assumption that the "I am" and the Not-I are absolute entities in their finitude and separation.

Any world-viewed is correlative to the world-view of the subjective mind in which and for which it is evident. A change in the former is, therefore, also a change in the latter. In characterizing its world, the subjective mind also characterizes its own standpoint.

The phenomenology of mind thus reveals the subjective mind as an ascent from lower to higher, or from immediate to mediated positions; this is the educational process of maturing. It is actual for us, the phenomenologists of the mind, but the subjective mind itself is aware only of each of its stations or phases. In belaboring or working at its object it is aware only of its correlation with it.

The reason why the concrete educational process is hidden from its subjective mind is its representational thinking. For itself it maintains its formal-logical identity in opposition to its object-images (Vorstellung).

§333 (§416)

The subjective mind is, therefore, finite and rational. Its self-certainty is identical with its uncertainty concerning its alien object.

It exists, however, also in truth and not merely in its certainties. Its truth is the concrete process of self-development through the self-criticism of all insufficient stations and limited standpoints. In exploding one certainty after another, it works uncomprehendingly towards its goal which is the truth: The certainty of itself is elevated to its truth.

"The subject must fill itself with objective content or value, and objective contents or values must gain subjective existence in it." (X. 261)

§334 (§417)

The main levels of the subjective individual mind toward the realization of its truth are: *Consciousness* of objects, consciousness of the *self*, and *comprehension* (Vernunft) in which the subjective mind knows itself as a totality determining all levels and phases of its conscious and self-conscious appearance as its own essential development.

§335

Sensuous consciousness is correlated to its world as *immediate experience*. I am a singular momentary "this" individual to whom appear in rapid, flickering changes, various and sundry qualitative contents. They are immediately transfused with my feeling; they seem attractive, repulsive, and so on.

The manifold contents are *relative* to one another: What appears big or small, far or near, up or down, depends on its relation to other things or movements; and they are subjective as tied to and conditioned by the organs for experiencing them.

Universal categories present in the immediacy of consciousness and its experienced world are: The singular "this something," the "now" in relation to "earlier" and "later," and the "here" of location.

These categories of the sensuous consciousness are extremely abstract and poor; as such they are in sharp contrast to the infinite qualitative wealth of the empirically concrete or immediate experience.

As soon as the sensuous consciousness becomes aware of this contradiction and of the abstract emptiness of those categories in which it must express its standpoint—"everything is a singular this, here, now" —it has ceased to be an immediate sensuous consciousness.

§338 (§421)

The dialectic inherent in this standpoint of empirical consciousness is at once also the dialectic of its finite objects.

On the one hand, perceptual consciousness clings to an empirical manifold of things ultimately real; on the other hand, they are negated and are classed under general concepts, which are *not* empirical things. Further, scientific objects, on the one hand, are unified through their general predicates; on the other hand, they are not unified, but torn apart as if they consisted of general matters (for example, sweetness, quietness, hardness, are such general matters assembled in a piece of sugar); thus, they form aggregates without a real unity.

In this *mixture* of empirical things and general classes, perceptual consciousness tumbles about, now declaring one side and then again the other side to be essential. It constantly contradicts itself: On the one hand, finite objects are essential and their general predicates unessential; on the other hand, the general features are essential and the particular thing only a case or illustration of them.

§339-340

For *reason* (Verstand) this self-contradiction is intolerable. It solves it by declaring perceptual, observable objects to be external appearances of their inner essential nature. It intends to replace the above mixture or composite by a genuine synthesis of universal logical forms—laws of nature—and given perceptual materials, determined by the laws of various abstract sciences.

"General laws of nature maintain their identity throughout the changes of observable events. An inner realm of laws quietly reigns in the turmoil of external appearances.

In such concepts as 'cause and effect' or 'energy and its manifestations,' reason postulates a necessary inner connection of outer appearances. For example, the law of planetary systems are united by a necessary non-appearing or inner unity in which reason finds its own law confirmed in external experience.

Universal objective rational world-order is correlative to reason." (X. 269)

§341

But reason does not comprehend what it has discovered. Its universal coherent or rational world-order is not identical with any one of its many laws; they are self-distinctions within a concrete ideal unity. Reason demands a complete, rational unity, but none of its natural laws fulfills this demand or postulate.

But a concrete unity, which makes such distinctions within itself, is no longer an object at all that can be kept over against the finite subject. The rational subject finds its own nature in the object, and the object behaves as if it were a subject. An absolute concrete unity distinguishes forms of unity within itself, which it both posits and transcends. The various laws of nature are partial unifications, which are real distinctions within the whole, without tearing this whole apart. The truth of reason, hence, of which reason is not aware, is nothing less than the speculative Concept: A subject which is absolutely objective, and an object which is absolutely subjective. . . . One, which distinguishes many forms of unity within itself, without losing its concrete dialectical identity in them.

"Reason is the highest level of object-thinking. Its false initial assumption of a subject thinking, on one side, and an object alien to it and thought about, on the other side, is an untenable contradiction. In the discovery of this contradiction, reason is driven beyond its standpoint to the concrete dialectical unity of opposites—in this case the unity of subject-object in the comprehensive self-consciousness of life.

In life, consciousness contemplates a process which develops its own essential distinctions as modifications of its own concrete identity. As such, life is its own final cause (Selbstzweck). It produces itself as a totality in which all self-produced functions are mutually serving one another to form a functional whole.

As aware of this dialectical living unity in its infinite self-differentiation, consciousness becomes self-consciousness. Self-consciousness is actual in the "I am" who knows itself objectively." (X. 272)

§342

This living actuality in the subject-object is its Concept (Begriff). It is speculative because it mirrors in itself a cosmic life which also is a concrete universality and self-differentiation. "I have thus in one and the same consciousness myself and my world; I find myself in my world and I find my world in myself; world-itself—that which *is*—gives me my objectivity and finds in me its subjectivity. This "I am" is the unity of I and objectivity or Being. This unity is spirit (Geist). As immediate, it is not yet developed; it must become for itself what it is in itself and attain its freedom." (X. 273)

§343

Life aware of itself is self-knowledge or Concept. It results from the dialectical negation of reason as object-thinking; or reason, in overcoming its finite contradiction of subject vs. object, becomes the comprehensive Concept.

§344

Self-consciousness—I am relating myself to myself —not only overcomes object-consciousness; it also preserves it as a necessary level or aspect of its concrete unity with itself and with its world.

The previous movements in the ascent of the mind are now understood as characterizing self-knowledge: Sensuous consciousness, perceptual experience, scientific object-thinking are also—although not known to themselves—the attitudes which spirit, in its freedom, has produced and chosen so as to express stations of its own development.

SELF-CONSCIOUSNESS

§345

The core of self-consciousness is its practical intentionality (Trieb) to actualize its potentiality, to *find* itself in *producing* itself.

§346 (§426)

Desire or appetite is the immediate form of this practical intentionality (Begierde). It practically denies the independence of sensuous objects: It uses, destroys, and consumes them for its own satisfaction. "It maintains itself by negating threatening negations of life." (X. 277) (For example, eating negates the threat of starvation.)

§347

The essential destiny of finite objects is: To be corroded and changed. Since they have no intentionality, they cannot ward off this destiny or put up a fight against anything which dissolves them. The practical activity of the I who uses them is therefore not an external abuse, for such actions conform to the very nature of finite objects. The practical subject, in its struggle with them, links itself to their externality and mortality.

§348

This destructive desire or appetite seeks its self-satisfaction; it is selfishness. The negation of felt wants, which is the fulfillment of selfishness, is singular and momentary and must constantly be renewed. No selfish satisfaction is lasting.

§349-350

In the destruction and use of given objects, which are helpless and selfless, the selfish subject beholds its own futility. The object is appropriated by a practical activity and thereby enters and becomes part of this subjective practical self; the subject, on the other hand, depends for its life on objects external to it. Its desire or appetite is determined and colored by the objects of desire by which it is externalized (entäussert).

§351

Being dissatisfied with the futility and negativity of its immediate satisfactions, the subjective mind rises above them. The immediate identity with its appetitive nature being broken, this *dissatisfaction* with its immediate satisfactions is a new and *mediated satisfaction*. One strives to rise above his natural immediacy and asserts himself as a free agent.

§352

The I, in conflict with its immediate practical existence (Dasein), is both individual and social. Every practical self is in the same situation, recognizing in the other the same problem which is in itself. The object of desire thus changes and becomes another I. Each I wants to be one with and *recognized* by another I; concurrently, each I remains an independent individual, an alien object for the other.

§353

The life of the subjective mind thus becomes a *struggle for recognition:* On the one hand, each is an internal struggle to gain mastery over its immediate appetitive existence, prove his freedom to himself, and produce a feeling of self-respect (Selbstgefühl); on the other hand, each is an external struggle to convince the other that it is worthy of his respect and recognition.

§354

This mutual struggle for recognition is mingled with the feeling of mistrust and uncertainty; it entails the dangerous risk, which every self-consciousness takes, when it dares to lay itself open to the other. If this life-and-death struggle (a colloquial expression) degenerates into a bloody fight in which one combatant is killed, the whole problem of recognition is missed; this is the raw elimination of the whole problem, which requires the preservation of immediate existence as a condition and sign of freedom.

§355 (§333)

The internal and external struggle of the self-conscious subjective mind is essentially a *struggle for freedom;* even though, in a complex historical situation, it permits the rise of masters and slaves. The subjection of the appetitive mind to serve the freedom of the higher self appears externally in dominion and servitude. Preferring immediate existence to freedom, the slave forfeits to be recognized as free; the master, in turn, is recognized as free, beholding in the slave the sign of his freedom.

Historically states arise in this group struggle for status. Factually, if a self-consciousness, absorbed in its immediate appetites, is to be elevated to a higher form of a common universal self-consciousness, this transition is unavoidable and relatively speaking justified. This historical start of political life is *merely* the external beginning in appearance; it is not the principle of a true state. For instance, "it is the limitation of ancient peoples that they have not recognized freedom as essential to every self-consciousness; that every man qua human is entitled to be free and to participate in a universal self-consciousness of all." (X. 286) *Mere might is never the ground of right.*

§356

Independent masters and dependent slaves form a *community*. To preserve and protect the life of his

216

workers becomes the concern of the master. Instead of an immediate destruction and consumption of singular objects of momentary appetites, objects are cultivated, preserved, and transformed by *work* in anticipation of a future which is the common concern of the whole community.

§357 (§435)

The servant learns to work. He acquires habits and skills. At the same time he disciplines himself. In forming objects, he also informs himself. In working together with others he overcomes his immediacy and is recognized in his excellence. In this process, the relation of dependence and independence is being reversed: The independent master becomes dependent on the skills and virtues of the servant.

"Having elevated himself over the selfish singularity of his natural will, the servant now ranks higher in value than the master, who merely beholds the shallow sign of his freedom in the servant. His lordship sinks to a mere formality.

Learning to obey another, in willing to give up selfish immediacy of appetites, is a necessary *origin of all true education.* No man who has not gone through this discipline, breaking his immediate egotism, can become free and worthy of command. The educator, on the other hand, works to make himself superfluous." (X. 288)

"The former master can only be free if the former slave is also free." (X. 290)

The fear of the lord is the beginning of wisdom. (Hegel's quotation from the Bible is witty—the "lord" has undergone a remarkable transformation!)

§358

Subjective mind actualizes its universal self-consciousness in the reciprocal recognition of the freedom and independence of the other and itself.

This mutuality and interdependence of voluntary recognition and respect is the substance of all communities—be they friendship, love, family, state, or church. *All virtues* are rooted in it; they are vices—hollow honor, vainglory—in isolation and separation from their substance.

§359

Comprehension (Vernunft), as existing in the subjective mind, is the concrete identity of its object-consciousness and its free self-consciousness.

§360

In this correlation of the consciousness of object with the consciousness of self, each side mutually characterizes the other: The *world-viewed* characterizes the *world-view* in and for which it is evident.

§361

Comprehension exists in and for itself in every mature individual. The *objective determinations* of the essential nature of things are known to be partly identical with the *subjective self-determinations* of thought.

§362

The subjective mind has thus reached its truth in Comprehension. Subjective mind, which knows truth and through which truth knows itself, is *spirit* (Geist).

§363

Spirit is the goal whereby the progression through the levels of the soul and subjective mind is known as progress and ascent. It is a movement towards, as well as within, spirit. Soul and mind are finite in every one of their stations: Soul is finite because it is immersed in natural life; consciousness is finite because it is correlated to finite objects of knowledge and desire. Spirit is the totality of all functions of soul and mind.

§364

Spirit as immediate unity of the finite soul and of the finite mind is still finite itself; it is its task to work out and to discover its infinity. The immediate finitude of spirit is the necessary prerequisite or obstacle overcoming which it become for itself what it is in itself: Free spirit.

§365

The spirit is progression in the consciousness of freedom towards its absolute self-fulfillment, leaving no opposites outside its totality. "The finite struggle of the spirit within and against its finitude is eternally willed and posited in the holy, blessed, absolute, and infinite spirit. The divine spirit is thus present in the human. The *infinite and eternal spirit* is completely *one with the non-absolute finite spirit,* which is forever distinguished from it as its own self-distinction." (X. 298)

§366

The way of liberation is the development of the spirit as free *theoretical* intelligence, and free *practical* will. These are two inseparable poles within its complete process.

§367

The struggle with theoretical and practical obstacles characterizes the whole sphere of finite subjective mind. "The theoretical function is no less an activity than the practical function (X. 305). It is therefore wrong to say that theory is passive or is only receiving given stuff, and that practice is active in producing works that did not exist before. Theory also produces such works as for example *language,* apart from which productivity nothing would be knowable; and practice also is determined by given contents which are dependent upon being known prior to acting upon them. Equally false is the preference for practical over theoretical activity, declaring intelligence to be conditional and will to be unconditional. Both are conditioned and unconditional. Practical will meets the resistance of objects and of other wills with which it is joined in battle; whereas free intelligence, realizing its intentions in language, remains one with its utterance and accomplishes a contemplative life which is divine and blessed in itself." (X. 396) These fallacies are examples of the general failure of rationalistic metaphysics, which divides the mind into separate compartments; and of empiristic psychology, which singles out and prefers one detail over another.

The whole ascent of the soul through mind and spirit is leading towards that *logic of truth* which is at the same time its *ontological basis.* If empiricism renounces this logical principle of understanding spirit, it remains confined to an indefinite manifold of details, to the untruth and illusions of the empirical natural soul, and to the peculiarities and idiosyncrasies of individuals.

§368

Willing and knowing, *heart* and *head* are dialectically interdependent. In and for spirit, the will with its purposes and interests is one content of knowledge; and knowledge is a content freely willed and chosen by the will to truth. In willing the truth, will renounces itself; it is its own self-determination to abstract from its interests, in contemplating them. There is no reason without will and no will without reason. This dialectic of subjectivity is the *Concept* of finite spirit: The self is the power to cancel, preserve, and unite its own opposite functions as fluid moments of its process of activity.

Pure subjectivity is knowledge in and for itself; it is its own object, which remains at the same time internal to itself.

Spirit is thus subject-object in and for itself. In distinction from object thinking or consciousness (Wissen), the self-conscious comprehensive knowledge (Erkennen) is a higher level, because its objectivity is inseparable from its subjectivity; or subjectivity is objectively real in and for itself." (X. 312)

This corresponds to Aristotle's "Dynamis" and "Entelechy": The former is the living potentiality; the latter is the activity which actualizes the subject as a being in becoming for itself what it is in itself. (§369-§378 traces the theoretical function of the whole subjective mind from its origin in the natural soul to the philosophical comprehension as it exists in finite minds. It corresponds to the four levels of logic—Hegel here admits that he has four, not three, levels—Being, Essence or reflection, Concept, Idea (§388-§399) traces the corresponding logical levels of the practical function of the same whole subjective mind.)

SUBJECTIVE MIND AS THEORETICAL

§369

The theoretical intelligence in the soul in its immediacy is a subconscious (dumpf) feeling interwoven with the life of nature, which furnishes all its materials (Stoff). On a conscious level, theoretical intelligence exists in a correlation of knowing attitudes with their intentional objects. On the level of self-consciousness, the two previous levels are known as self-determinations of the whole mind. All levels are actual in individuals.

§370

Finite subjective mind as a whole is the source of all its knowledge, including sensuous knowledge of immediate experience. Nothing, therefore, is more false than the empiristic prejudice that nothing can be in the mind that was not first in the senses. On the contrary, nothing can be in the senses, unless there is a sentient and feeling mind. The same criticism holds for the subjectivistic irrationalism which derives all knowledge from immediate moments and inner feelings. This is indeed the natural soul in its immediacy; but as such it is private and not communicable. It is an abstraction from community. To appeal to one's immediate feeling, therefore, renders impossible any comprehensive communication: I cannot feel what you feel, you cannot feel what I feel, there is no knowledge whatsoever which we could impart. We must leave each person to his private isolated exclusiveness.

In all actual knowledge, there is no feeling by itself; feeling is only in correlation with contents that are felt: "In dealing with the soul, we have spoken about feeling as an awakening in which its break and its unity with its subconscious sleeping natural life is felt. On the level of consciousness, the feeling of the subject was treated in correlation with felt qualities in the object. On the level of self-consciousness, the total subjective mind feels itself as totality in all its functions; the subject makes its functions its own felt objects." (X 315) I feel my feelings of love or hate for or against their intentional objects to be objectively there in me.

As consciously directed towards its intentional object, feeling develops into a definite sensitivity for such objects (Empfindung); it pays attention and is attention. "In paying attention, I forget myself in the situation and let the situation unfold itself in and for me" (die Sache walten lassen).

"This emotional and passionate attention to the values and concerns of objective situations contains germinally the whole content of comprehension. All object-images, concepts, and thoughts concerning nature and the spirit develop out of this intentional sensitivity. Spiritual values of morality, right, and religion are born in feeling, and after their complete explication and interpretation, they again return and are concentrated in the simple form of passionately felt convictions." (X. 317)

In the further process of knowing, subjective mind proceeds to cancel its immediate unity with felt contents and distinguishes its own feelings and qualities qua felt from objects stripped and deprived of feeling. This is *representational object-thinking* (Vorstellung).

Representational thinking is the act of looking at its objects, locating them externally in space and time, and comparing them with what it remembers of them in abstract generalized images. They are external to the immediate occurring events which were perceived and from which they are abstracted.

"Reason is, on the one hand, sunk in given stuff. On the other hand, it remembers itself as opposed to this, its own externality—'I have seen this before.' It does not comprehend itself as a complete dialectical process." (X 327).

§374

Representational object-images, which seem to disregard empirical occurrences and to be exempt from time, nevertheless are *located* in the spatio-temporal *subject* who produces them. It possesses them as contents of its own knowledge. They are integrated and placed within a general "I think."

§375

Due to their emancipation from empirical perceptions, generalized images may represent any content anywhere or at any time. This is *reminiscence*. Reminiscence bestows *duration* on its contents. "What is not thus preserved merely passes, is gone, and is forgotten. Reminiscence is a storehouse of remembered treasures. But this advantage is also a loss: General object-images lose the clarity and freshness of a concrete intuition, which is fully determined in all of its aspects and is present as an individual totality. They are blurred in the general image.

In our perceiving life, time is short when many changing contents are present; long, when lack of variety reminds us of the boredom of our empty subjectivity, when monotony is interrupted by nothing. Time is short when we are busy with many contents; long, when our interests and activity is occupied with few objects of interest (X 332)."

§376

Reproductive imagination goes further in idealizing object-images, divesting them of their status in empirical contexts. It produces them freely and spontaneously, and combines them in new ways, independent of their original context in space and time. This idealization must not be confused with a purely empirical association of ideas, where one image leads to another, as in dreaming or daydreaming. Rather, many similar images are condensed. They are attracted to one another by the power of the imagination, in which the I sees, grasps, and condenses its own images.

"This power of imagination is an inner light which disperses the nightly darkness, covering the treasure of its images; it steps out of its inwardness and banishes vagueness through the lightful clarity of its presence." (X. 337)

§377

If images are used to express the subjective mind in its universality—the same in you and in me—reproductive imagination becomes *productive expressive imagination* or fantasy; it is the fertile ground for poetic symbols and allegories.

Image as outer impression now fuses with image as inner expression; it is the symbolic fusion of inner and outer. Art expresses the true universal activity of mind, the Idea, in the sensuous presence of an image (Dasein).

§378-§382

(The key term of these §§ is "Gedächtnis." Hegel informs us in a footnote to §379 that he does not use it in the dictionary meaning of "memory," but he does not say in which meaning he does use it. My guess is that he uses it in connection with the verb "gedenken." I therefore translated it by "thoughtfulness.")

Thoughtfulness (Greek mnemosyne) is the mother of the muses; it transforms symbolic images into *signs.* Images now signify or mean something which has no resemblance to them, as a flag is the allegorical sign of a country.

Subjective mind thus creates *language,* a learned and remembered system of communication through visible or audible signs.

Reproductive and productive imagination fuse in an interplay mediated through language. Language is both subjective and objective. It is the objective medium in which subjective minds can meet. Subjective minds create and fill their own space and time with this transparent and self-produced reality.

If language is used mechanically by rote (auswendig) and thoughtlessly, then that which originally was thoughtfulness degenerates into a thinking machine.

§383

The thoughtfulness of language makes thinking possible: We can *think objectively* and validly when we can rely on terms, the meaning of which we understand and share.

§384

Thought is the identity of subjective understanding and objective understood content. What is thought, is; what is, exists in and for thought.

§385

In its immediacy, thought is tied to object-images (Vorstellung). Herein subjective minds and given images, singular contents and general forms *fall apart.*

§386

As *reason,* thought clings to its formal identity over against that which is different from it. Reason makes the original distinction (Ur-Teil) between itself and that which it is not. The comprehensive Concept thinks this process of reason as a symbolic unity of opposites. As such a concrete and struggling process, reason does not only identify objects but is a self-determining actuality.

In the *Logic*, thinking has been considered first as being-in-itself; second, in its dialectical essence corresponding to self-reflection; third, as Concept, wherein dialectic exists not only in itself but also for itself; and finally, as eternal process in all its essential moments or as Idea.

These categories of the *Logic* appear again in the medium of the soul as levels of its development: As immediate subjectivity, as awake and conscious, as self-conscious, and as comprehensive. The difference is the difference of the logical and the non-logical medium; but the different media are opposite manifestations of one and the same Absolute.

§387

Subjective mind grasps in its own comprehensive Concept its core and absolute content. The soul thus actualizes its true nature and becomes a free mind as well as a free will.

"Without true thought, there is no free will; and without the free choice to think, there is no true thought. An animal cannot have a will, but only desires because it does not think." (X. 364)

SUBJECTIVE MIND AS PRACTICAL

§388-§390

(§388-§390 now develops the corresponding levels of self-conscious spirit as practical.) Spirit as will knows itself as that which decides for itself and fulfills itself in self-chosen tasks. The problem of the finite will is to work out its freedom or self-determination. Will is in agreement with itself when it embraces existential purposes as its own. This is its freedom, the final cause of all finite purposes. Finite will moves towards these goals, struggling with its momentary impulses and interests, thus achieving its end: Freedom. In this process, Finite mind achieves this goal in morality, law, and social ethics, which are concrete universals, dependent on thought.

The existing soul in its individual immediacy is practical feeling. This inward feeling or "heart" is the will of all actions.

Feeling, will, and thought are in one comprehensive process. It is just as foolish (töricht) to hold on to the inward immediacy of feeling against objective moral and ethical problems, as it is to deny that these problems remain soaked with feeling and return to feeling." (X. 268f)

Against abstractions of reason, feeling may appear as a totality; but if feeling is set up in its immediacy against objective values, it also may be one-sided, unessential contingent, "subjective" in the bad sense of private whim or smug vanity, refusing to enter a concrete and rational community of discourse. (§370)

§391

Practical feeling implies anticipation of what *ought* to be (sollen). The feeling of *pain* is produced by a felt inadequacy or disproportion between what is and what ought to be. If that which ought to be definitely fails, then this failure is felt as *evil*. All levels of practical life as finite existence are permeated by feelings of pain, evil, and suffering. In its immediacy, the lack of correspondence between the objects of desire and the desires themselves is felt as unpleasant or disagreeable.

There are innumerable forms and *levels of the*

ought. Evil, besides being a disappointing failure or non-fulfillment of an ought, is secondly a preference of a lower to a higher level of the ought.

Evil is unavoidable: Without desire, will, affirmation of values, there would be no evil, nothing undesirable, no negation of value. Each self must negate the threatening negativity directed against its practical existence and freedom. Its demand upon itself and upon the world originates evil; only if I expected truth can I suffer lies as evil. Only the dead know no evil and pain.

"In relation to my immediate vital self-interest, evil is the disagreeable and unpleasant absence of particular means vital to my self-preservation; or the presence of a threatening negation of the same. In relation to important concerns and objective duties, this vital feeling of pleasant or unpleasant, agreeable or disagreeable becomes unimportant and peripheral; it is replaced by the deeper pain of anguish and disappointment in the moral worth of man.

Feelings of joy, hope, fear, dread, sorrow, all rank above the class of immediate vital feelings. They belong to the realm of personal relations either internally, when a person makes demands on himself, or externally, when he expects good actions of other persons.

Contentment and serenity are quiet affections and lasting feelings when a person has succeeded in bringing his affairs in agreement with his feeling of self-respect.

In terror, the unexpected impact of a brutal world is suddenly felt as a shock, threatening my whole self-existence.

The highest feelings are related to the moral, ethical (*sittlich*), and religious ought. In shame and repentance, inadequacy in regard to duty and the better self is felt; and this feeling is the actual beginning of the undoing of one's wrongdoing. The empirical regret is a caricature of repentance: One regrets the good action because it turned out to have disagreeable consequences for him.

"The great man and sterling character achieves a quiet, contemplative (besonnen) feeling; he suffers misfortune without being overwhelmed by sorrow, and he experiences a harmony between his will and his achievement without breaking out in self-congratulatory applause; he has laid aside his vanity and feels no need to emphasize and to tell the world that it is he—this empirical individual—who is successful or unsuccessful." (X. 371)

§392

The moral ought checks and cancels the immediate subjectivity of feeling in which it arose. The natural soul in its immediacy resents and objects to this moral necessity to which it is subjected and to which it subjects itself. An unfree and passive life of pleasure likes simply to *find* given objects agreeable to its immediate desires; and dislikes to work for them and to work at itself.

The ought is the beginning of an infinite series of intentional acts. Since practical acts must always be done in a here and now, the whole intentionality (Trieb) of the soul to realize its freedom, is a contradiction to the restricted, bounded situations of all practical life. *Pathos* (Leidenschaft) is the expression of this contradiction; man throws himself wholly into a cause which does not deserve such a whole-hearted, passionate devotion; practical life is pathetic. The whole subjectivity of the individual is absorbed by particular determinations of the will.

§393

Passion as such is neither good nor bad; it depends on the objective worth of the cause which it serves (§94). Passion is a form of practical existence where an individual identifies himself wholly with his cause. His vitality, his character, and his talents are called out and drawn upon to achieve his satisfaction. "Nothing great has been accomplished without passion, or could it be accomplished; only a deadly hypocritical moralism condemns a passionate life as evil." (X, 374)

This is the paradox of the will: It is free *from* the selfish ego and *for* comprehensive values, with which it identifies itself; at the same time that it *has to rely* on the selfish natural ego; the latter must be preserved as the living agent, precisely as it must be transcended.

The self seeks the good, but the good also seeks the self to be its agent. Further, the self seeks the good in many conflicting directions; thus many inclinations, urges, passions, and duties are in unavoidable collision, both in the discreet person and in his relation to other finite wills. Since they cannot all be satisfied, they imply *resignation*, and are mutually restrictive. Practical life is never an unmixed blessing.

"This is Plato's idea of justice, to assign to every value its due share in the self-realization of the whole spirit. But this is true not merely in and for the objective shape of justice in the state, as he puts it, but it is also true for every subjective finite soul." (X. 376)

The individual must take an *interest* in what he does. Without being driven by interests there would be no activity; likewise without objective and shared values there would be no direction to vital interests— left to themselves, they would be chaotic. "Universal ethical values as such do no act; only subjective agents act and they act with interest and passion.

This paradoxical necessity that the spirit must rely on the very self which it seeks to overcome must not be confused with selfishness, the latter pre-

231

fers the lower natural wishes of self to the higher spiritual values of self-determination and self-respect.

Morality and duty are not merely opposed to individual interests; they are also united with them. The individual must be preserved even in concerns of the highest order." (X. 377)

§395

This moral dialectical of universal ends and finite agents, of many conflicting intentionalities and passions, prompts ethical reflection on what constitutes the good and blessed life (Glückseligkeit).

§396

Practical life is a life of sacrifice; since it is impossible to fulfill all intentions, some must be sacrificed for others. The choice rests ultimately on the subject's feeling what would be good, even though his calculations of value may give it rational justification.

§397

Practical life, thus, consists in the ever-renewed freedom of definite choices. An infinite universal negativity pervades it, whereby no choice, no hope, no expectation is not ultimately disappointed. But to live in this absolute uncertainty is necessary. Man cannot choose not to choose, or will not to will. The concrete totality of the practical spirit encloses and preserves all choices as individual moments of its life.

§398

To affirm practical life as this infinite dialectical and complete self-contradiction is the actuality of the good. In affirming practical life as infinite struggle, the finite will comes into agreement with its infinite essence. This essential agreement with itself is spiritual freedom in itself as well as for itself.

"The good, therefore, is not merely that which ought to be; what ought to be is included in the total affirmation of the struggle as a whole, which absolutely is as it ought to be; it cannot be different from what it is. To demand that it ought to be different is a refusal to accept practical actuality—a futile escape!

The free spirit, in realizing his true and necessary situation, has gone beyond finite actions and particular purposes. The good is identified with the dialectical and universal truth of practical life. This truth of practice in its totality transcends the practical. Freed from short-sided perspectives, the contemplative Concept of the good life alone sets man actually free. He does not merely *have* the Idea of freedom: He *is* it, in it and through it." (X. 379f)

(This is Hegel's *tragic heroism*. Let us look back: The *soul* is an immediate struggle between sanity and insanity, rampant irrational vitality and abstract moralism. The demands of the *subjective mind* on itself and on the world creates a felt discrepancy between what ought to be and what is—on all practical levels of life. Practical existence is pervaded by *pain* in all its value-dimensions; it is a life of sacrifice, of unavoidable collisions, disillusions, and disappointments—and what is the ethical conclusion? The whole of this utterly *problematic struggle* is unconditionally affirmed and this unconditional affirmation of practical activity is the *actuality of the good:* Practical life as a whole is as it ought to be, and cannot be different from what it is—namely this finite problematic struggle between what ought to be and what is. In this free acceptance of necessity, in this inevitable negativity or freedom, man finds himself accepted and justified in turn. To live and affirm life, not in spite of but because it is hard and painful, is the infinite value of every individual. This is the ethical refutation of any idyllic epicureanism, which defines the good as the absence of evil; and is in line, as Hegel says (X, 380), with the ethical core of the Christian religion.)

OBJECTIVE MIND

(The objective mind is the second level of the finite spirit. The second edition expands the two brief paragraphs §400-401 into an introduction of five paragraphs §482-487; lecture notes of the fourth edition add concrete valuable illustrations.)

INTRODUCTION

In subjective spirit there is always a cleavage between moral demands—the ought—and the contingencies of immediate interests. As an objective actual process, this struggle is what it ought to be. Objective mind, then, is a unity of theoretical, logical structures—and finite subjective wills as its agents. In the objective mind theoretical wholes are *willed* and subjective wills are *thought* as being contained, directed and sustained by such intelligible systems of co-operation.

The state with its constitution, laws, governmental agencies, parties and all individual citizens is such a system, for example. The state must be *thought* and can exist only in and for thought. Its totality must be in the *mind* of all citizens. But it also must be *willed* by all. It is actual only in the individual loyalty of its members. The state, thus, exemplifies objective mind as unity of theoretical intelligence and practical will, wherein individuals gain their freedom and maturity in co-operative, objective, or shared forms of practice. Objective forms of freedom shape an actual world into which the individual is born. They appear to the newcomer and are felt by him as objective connections and powers which he cannot but acknowledge in their validity or value (Gelten). Laws, for example, have an objective authority, no less than generally accepted *morals* and *customs* of a people.

In all manifestations of the objective mind there are correlations of duties and rights:

The duty of parents to nurture and educate their children corresponds to the right of the child to be nurtured and educated.

The right to possess property is correlative to a duty to administer it properly as a means of personal freedom and a sign of personal worth. To respect the property of others, therefore, is showing respect for them as responsible persons in charge of their property.

The right of governments to enforce the law is correlative to their duty to act within the law and to administer it justly.

The Concept of the objective mind is the concrete interplay or dialectical unity of all the spheres of rights and duties: Such as the family, social-professional groups and institutions, political administrative functions; and such as personal morality, legality of public transactions, and political ethics.

(Critics who either have not read Hegel or are not able to read him have sneered that he has no ethics but only a philosophy of law or legality. They have overlooked his usual trick; in §486 of the second edition, Hegel says, "The existing reality of the free will is Right (Recht) *which must not be taken in the limited sense of jurisprudence, but in a comprehensive sense embracing all existing determinations of freedom*"—a very large assignment for a term which ordinarily is understood only in that legal sense which Hegel forbids!)

LEGALITY

§402-403 (§488)

In the sphere of law the individual subject or the subjective mind is a free *person* who knows that he is entitled to this freedom by right. He acquires a legal objectivity, which he gains through the possession of external things as property. Apart from this, freedom, in its immediacy, would be an abstract and empty title.

§404 (§489)

The practical activity whereby I make an external thing my own, means that I identify my will with my *property*. I loan my will to something that has no will of its own. It thereby becomes a means for an end which is the legally recognized existence of the person.

§405-406 (§490-491)

Property mediates the person with himself and with other persons. Although it remains external to the self, it is nevertheless acknowledged by himself and by others as belonging to a free person: He is respected when his property is respected. This respect is mutual and is the foundation for a legal *community* in which personal rights are secured. Mediated through property, will has a knowable, definite, and publicly recognized existence in a community of mutually free and independent persons. Something becomes property either through direct *acquisition,* or through making or *forming* it, or through a *legal title*.

§407 (§492)

Since things have no right of their own and are external to will, there is freedom to keep them or not to keep them. With the person's will and consent he can surrender them to another who is willing and consenting to own them: The *contract*.

§408 (§493)

The contract is a *valid deed* when one person expressly stipulates his willingness and conditions thereof, to surrender his property to another, and when the other has accepted this stipulation. This *public transaction* completes the contract and makes it objectively valid. Its validity does not depend on its actual fulfillment, because the act of doing or performing may go on in an indefinite division of time and work; nor does its validity depend on the person's moral worth, because the contract need not consider motivations of the inner self—for instance, the contract is indifferent as to whether these motivations are honest or deceptive. Rather than testing the moral qualities of wills, it regulates external transactions.

§409 (§494)

The property has specific personal qualities for the owner. These are disregarded in contracts, wherein different qualities are compared solely in terms of depersonalized, abstract exchange value. Such is *money*, a quantitative, equal, general measure.

§410 (§495)

On account of his identification with his property, or insofar as one identifies his will with his possessions, can he be coerced. Personal freedom is thus vulnerable.

Subjective will may or may not conform to objective right; it may even break it and thus produce wrong. This arbitrary disregard of right, however, does not annul its objective validity. Right remains real in and for itself, and it *ought* to be maintained. While conflict of right and wrong is unavoidable, since the objective and public and the subjective and private aspects of the will are inseparable opposites, the right nonetheless remains objectively valid.

§411 (§496)

The ambiguity of the will in itself and between many wills implies the necessity for *public arbitration.* In such public conflicts over right and wrong, each party pleads for its case and has legal arguments on its side. The judge must rightly assume that in each case only one solution can be the right one. This assumption clashes with the opposite assumption that each of the opposite parties argues for its right. What is right in itself—the assumption of the judge—is not identical with the apparent conflict of rights (Schein des Rechts).

§412 (§497)

This uncertainty of who is right and the legal claims and defenses of each party against the other in civil law suits could not take place if the objectivity of the right in and for itself were not presupposed. The *judge* must represent this objectivity of right. This requires his independence from practical interests, if he is to judge them impartially.

§413 (§498)

A just judgment is not *coercion.* If the party accepts it as just, even though it may go against his interests, he confirms his freedom and self-determination. In the acceptance of such a verdict against a person, his dignity and freedom are recognized.

When the person himself is violated, whether in the breaking of contract or whatever, action becomes *crime.* Criminal actions pursue their interests regardless of right through coercion and lies. Thus in distinction from contract, crime involves the motivation of the will. The will is *evil* (böse) when a purely subjective illusory right (Schein des Rechts) is pursued in violation of the absolute right of free persons to be respected as ends in themselves.

§414 (§500)

Practical reason as abstract and general makes negative demands: "Thou shalt not!" These abstract moral imperatives engender what they forbid. For example, if there were no imperative "thou shalt not kill," killing would not be murder—a crime; as indeed there are no crimes in nature.

But crime does not only violate abstract moral laws. In violating the right of others, criminal action violates the concreteness of a common life and turns life into an enemy. In its immediacy, this hostility of violated life appears as *revenge.* Revenge or retaliation, however, as immediate action against crime, is not better than crime itself. It leads to an endless progression of violence, to a vicious circle of crime and revenge.

As the uncertainty of right-claims in the sphere of property required an impartial judge, so the irrational action and reaction of crime and revenge requires an impartial *punishment.*

And as the partner of a broken contract restores his integrity in momentarily accepting a legally valid fine, so does the criminal restore his integrity as a free moral person in momentarily accepting his punishment as an objective and just *repentence.*

§415

This development of right goes beyond the legal sphere of right; right transcends itself in *morality.* The moral standpoint is reached when the free person identifies his subjective will with an objective and universal moral law; or when a universal law becomes his will. The person achieves his moral status when he affirms himself in negating his isolated subjectivity.

The expression "natural right" is ambiguous. Man is not "good by nature" as if he could not help but be good (a positive axiological determinism). This doctrine directed against the equally false position that man is "evil by nature" or "totally depraved" (a negative axiological determinism). Both extremes imply the abrogation of freedom and of right. The term "nature" is also used in the sense of "essential nature" or Concept of morality. In this sense, it is identical with moral freedom or self-determination which is a plus of determination beyond natural determination. Man determines himself by his universal moral law of freedom, in addition to what he is naturally.

That which is to be sacrificed and restricted is not the freedom of persons and their rights but the arbitrariness and violence of natural subjectivity, the so-called "state of nature."

MORALITY

§416 (§503)

Morality is a necessary and objective standpoint of the free subject. It includes a regard for the welfare of others in its own purpose. The moral will combines its good intention with intelligent insight into the need and the character of others. The universal will which is objectively valid in and for itself nevertheless is nothing outside of its activity in and through natural and subjective minds. This implies a dialectical contradiction in the moral will: On the one hand, it requires that I should overcome my subjective private interests; on the other hand, that I should include and care for them. The moral will insists on living this contradiction.

"The moral freedom of the subject is the core of all freedom, as it is understood in Europe. Man must know the distinction of good and bad as his own conviction. Ethical as well as religious self-determinations ought not to be enforced by external laws or dictates of authority. They ought to be followed because they are assented to, acknowledged by, and founded in the heart, good will, conscience, and insight of the moral subject. This objective subjectivity of the moral will is an absolute and essential end in itself." (X. 392)

§417

Corresponding to the inner dialectic of the moral will is an external one: On the one hand, only that deed which lays in one's intention can be imputed to him, can be his fault; on the other hand, he is concurrently held responsible for the consequences of his action, which were not foreseen in his intention. The consequences of his action may pervert his intention in unforeseen consequences in the world. The moral subject, thus, is in a vise between his good will and an objective moral world-order beyond his will.

§418 (§505)

This perennially restored contradiction drives the moral man to seek the unity of the objective world-order in conformity with the subjective moral purpose, and the moral purpose in conformity with the world-order. This search is the origin of incessant and never-successful activity.

Internally, it is the attempt to harmonize the right of the good will with the right of happiness or welfare. Private wishes and desires for happiness are the empirically manifold content of the good will. When good will is harmonized with the universal form of moral intention, happiness is justified.

§419

The center of morality does not lie in the objective world-order; the latter has no moral self which can be held responsible. It becomes morally important mainly in its perverting function, by which the activity of the subject is drawn into a whirl of consequences not meant or intended by the agent.

§420 (§507)

The unconditional good life is not an abstraction outside of individual, conditioned agents through whose particular wills, intentions, activities, and struggles alone it is actual.

Herein arises the *profoundest contradiction of morality:* The absolute and concrete unity of the good life is absolutely present in all parties in the collision of many conceptions of the good and in many conflicting duties. Every duty is absolute, but it is also in conflict with other duties which are equally absolute. This is the dialectic of the moral world that actions ought to agree and also that they ought to disagree. The totality of the good life is unimpaired by these contradictions.

§422 (§509)

The moral subject as finite must seek many satisfactions and must fulfill many duties. None of these can be said to be unconditionally good; often they are in conflict.

The finite subject becomes *evil* when it confuses the concrete universality of the good with his own particular cause. No finite will has the right to absolutize itself, but it has the freedom to choose this pseudo-absolute illusion and thus pervert the good into evil.

§423 (§510)

The *perversion of the good,* and value-blindness, does not invalidate the absolute value of the moral subject. The subject ought to prefer the higher to the lower value; also he ought note the distinction between its finite action and the infinite value of the same; he ought to accept the inevitable dialectic between that which it is and which it ought to be, and the fact that they always fall apart.

In this finite dialectic of the will, the good man may be unfortunate, the bad man fortunate, or vice versa. This does not imply, however, that the evil, which is futile and vain in itself, should not be resisted.

§424 (§511)

The private welfare or happiness of the individual ought to be pursued because it belongs to the wholeness of existence; and ought not to be pursued because it is not—as duty, right, and the good will are—an absolute end in itself. The ought thus is divided in itself; and it ought not be divided in itself, but ought to be harmonized, because the moral subject as a whole is a concrete idea of individuality and universality.

The many-sided contradiction of the ought must be decided from moment to moment by the individual. This constant responsibility of choice is his *conscience,* the core of freedom or morality.

At the same time, this profound and responsible freedom is also the possibility of irresponsibility. The individual as arbiter may arbitrarily pit his subjective decision against the good and may pretend to be master of the good, knowing himself to be bound or obligated to nothing. If this moment of negativity is isolated and set against all objective contents, freedom becomes license: The *principle of the bad.*

Due to the dialectical contradictions in the ought and in freedom, it is absolutely uncertain and contingent whether a good man is rewarded with happiness or not, whether a bad man is successful in the world or not. But the moral world-order ought to be such that good actions can be rewarded in it and that crimes should meet their deserved punishment; what is nil in itself should be annihilated.

The infinity of the moral subject manifests itself both in conscience, which may decide on a total sacrifice on behalf of the good and in its infinite irresponsibility, which may decide on a total abstraction from all objective values. The *all-sided contradiction of the moral ought* in the individual *constitutes* its pure, infinite, unpredictable, subjective *existence*. The bad will is an immediate perversion and self-annihilation of this existence; as external action, it is crime (§414).

§429

The good will (Gesinnung), on the contrary, negates the negative, naughts the naughty, and thus affirms its identity with the universal and objective good which it has freely chosen to serve. This objective good is the cause of all who serve it. The moral subject thus passes from the more restricted standpoint of morality to a more comprehensive perspective of social ethics (Sittlichkeit).

SOCIAL ETHICS (SITTLICHKEIT)

§430

Social ethics is the peak of the objective mind. Both the legal person and the moral subject function within it and are abstractions from it; they function within concrete finite objectively organized wholes of life. The freedom of the legal person mediated by external relations of material good, and the freedom of the moral subject mediated in itself and for itself as well as in relation to other moral subjects: In the concrete actuality of social ethics—commonly practiced and accepted habits and morals (Sitte)—are preserved and practiced within political freedom—a second nature. Political freedom is identical with a comprehensive general will, actual in all wills which know and determine themselves, mediated by a national constitution. The good will of the individual in its immediacy is in abstract opposition to social ethics, which is concrete. The good will matures, however, by participating in such social wholes. "Subjective freedom is incomplete if freedom is not universally practiced and respected, and the comprehensive freedom in a state knows itself in the consciousness and conscience of all individual citizens." (X. 397).

§431

What ought to be and what is are always in tension (§424) in the finite moral subject. The actuality of freedom politically guaranteed by the state for the whole people, is what it ought to be; freedom, then, is both the formed *substance* of a national life and its *final cause* (Absoluter Endzweck §197).

The individual is grounded in and gains his meaning through participation in the substantial life of the nation. Apart from this, the individual is accidental. This is his own present world. The social world into which individuals enter is an already accomplished substantial fact; on the other hand, the social world depends on all individual inner activities for its renewal. The individual finds concrete duties and social situations, which are what they are, before he entered them and which offer opportuni-

245

ties and demand fulfillments. The individual, in grasping those opportunities and fulfilling those demands of the situation, appropriates them as his own, makes himself essential to them, and stands for their moral necessity, which he practices as his own choice and freedom.

§432

Concrete social wholes condition and make possible the integrity of the individual to be for himself and to take care of his own affairs; concurrently, the whole is the common product of all individual inner activities through which alone it comes about. The independence of individuals and their dependence on a common social work are produced together and are producing each other: The welfare of the whole means the welfare of its members and the converse. To know this and to be loyal to it is the mutual *trust* which is the substantial core of social ethics. It implies that freedom for all and freedom for each are inseparable.

§433

The general work and labor, which is the substantial life of a people, is particularized in professions, social institution, and political differentiations (*Stände:* Station, profession, condition of things, class, rank, estates of a realm). The statesman cares for and is in charge of constitutional organizations of the political whole. Professions mediate common needs in division of labor, and in mutual exchange. The family elevates the natural individual into a spiritual bond. These general, particular, and individual functions of the objective mind depend on one another; *to respect the integrity of their different spheres is an essential principle of social ethics.*

"To fulfill one's station in social life is doing

246

one's duty, by which virtue or excellence is acquired. Social ethics rest on this ability to sacrifice oneself, to do justice to an objective situation, and to cultivate a benevolent mutual trust." (X, 398).

§434-§435

(These short paragraphs introduce the theme of the *family* and social excellence. They are expanded in the second edition to five paragraphs, §518-§522. I follow, under the above §434 of the first edition, the expanded treatment of the second edition without segmentation in the §§ numbers.)

The *family* is the objective spiritual bond, which links man and woman in mutual love, confidence, and respect. The sexual-natural differentiation is preserved in the ethical integrity of their objective and publicly recognized oneness; marriage is constituted both in the subjective feelings, as well as in this substantial unity. The exclusive wholeness and undivided dedication to one another constitutes a marriage as *monogomy*. Sexual intercourse in such a relation signifies a total dedication of each whole person to the other; each shares the personal interests of the other.

The *property* of the family, which is a common product and concern, is lifted above a mere formal legal status—as it had in the contract, regulating public transactions—and acquires a social-personal value.

Natural birth of children is spiritualized in that the parents have the duty to care and *educate* them so that they may become free persons; and the children have the right to be cared for and educated (§401).

The natural life of the family is one of intimate affection and feeling, in which the children are loved simply because they are children. In contradistinction, the ethical meaning of a concrete family-life is that it is a transition: Children are destined to acquire in and through it their independence, and have the right and duty to leave it. The natural life of the family is thus shown to be subordinated to its ethical meaning; it is transcended in that the children grow out of it by means of it. The death of the parents also illustrates natural contingency and brings about legal relations in the inheritance and transfer of family properties to new families. Brothers and sisters find themselves reduced to legal persons in legal property relations of the contractual type.

§436

In a business-society each member works for his own welfare. He also contributes involuntarily to a universal exchange of goods and services which lies as a whole beyond his individual planning and private interest.

The atomistic outlook of the business man in its immediacy loses sight of the ethical substance of the community; he understands the latter only in an analogy to his formal legal business contracts as an external state, which is merely there to guarantee the safety of business transactions.

§437 (§523-528)

The developed totality of business and labor organizes itself in complete professional groups. Each represents professional ethical codes and each is represented by individual agents in which alone those codes are actual. Such concrete laws are effective, as a second nature composed of habits and accepted customs or standards of the groups.

The universal exchange of socially organized practical functions is the work of the whole, in which the individual shares the profits and towards which he contributes his share and care. "Individual satisfactions are mediated through the work of all." (X. 401)

Ethical culture (Bildung) exists in the individual so far as he makes himself fit to take place in a social professional pattern; and to achieve his recognition as co-operating with others in common concerns. This is integrity (Ehre) and rightness (Rechtschaffenheit).

While division of labor, on the one hand, is the precondition for such social value or virtue of the individual; on the other hand, it leads to greater and greater socializations of functions, dependent more and more on impersonal connections. Skills thus become more and more mechanical and replaceable like machines.

§438

Formal laws abstractly formulate the general will, whereas actual laws are organically articulate in living customs and professional morals. When this organic ethical life is threatened and disrupted by natural impulses of individuals or by arbitrary subjectivity, abstract law goes into play; The governmental agencies in power enforce them and punish lawlessness or license. The general will, thus, ceases to be abstract and is enacted by individual agents who represent the government, entrusted with authority; personal and responsible decision must be made by them.

(Hegel seems to identify here "government" with a "prince"—Fürst).

He expresses a personal preference for a constitutional monarchy. But in other places he distinguishes this, his own personal preference, from his political philosophy: "Democracy, aristocracy, monarchy, are equally necessary functions in the history of the state." (X. 420)

"It is unessential for the Concept of the state whether those in power are many or one, whether several or one executive is elected, or whether the authority is entitled to his position of majesty by birth." (Deutsche Reichsverfassung, p. 16).

§439

The *constitution* stipulates that comprehensive will, which is actual in the understanding and loyalty of all citizens. It legitimately protects all particular branches of the national political organism against both arbitrary encroachments of the government as well as equally arbitrary lawlessness of individuals and mobs.

"Since the objective mind is *finite*, it is a vain utopian opinion to expect a perfect empirical state or a perfectly just political life." (X. 403)

"Positive laws may be just or unjust. Their amendments and further specifications are an endless process, a bad infinity." (X. 404)

The minimal rationality is this, that laws must be public and known to all citizens (X.404)

Those authoritarians who blindly rely on the fatherliness of benevolent despotism, appealing to the divine right of kings or to the natural love and obedience of their political subjects, reduce political life to nature—nature also is governed by laws, but unconsciously so. Laws regulating human affairs must be known by all, must be affirmed and acknowledged, even though they are necessarily mixed up with natural contingency or irrationality. (X. 404)

Anarchists, on the contrary, use the imperfections of political institutions to demand the abrogation of law and order—but the bad state is still better than no state at all. (X. 405)

The dialectical contradiction between public and common rationality of laws and the uncertainty of positive laws requires an independent judiciary branch of government in order to safeguard freedom within right and right within freedom (X. 406);

250

and a potential breaking of the laws requires a police force authorized to enforce laws." (X. 408)

"Freedom and equality before the law may rightly be said to be ultimate aims of any constitution. But one must not abstractly oppose them against the organic and concrete articulation of political life in the state; in it there is a necessary inequality and distinction of political functions. An abstract *equalitarianism* would make it impossible for a state to function.

The current formula, "all men are created equal, by nature," is ambiguous; it confuses the natural aspect of man with the Concept of freedom. By nature all men are unequal. Even the first and most abstract manifestation of freedom is already nonnatural: It is the recognition of the free person rightfully entitled to equal protection as owner of his property. More concretely, freedom is the moral law recognizing each man as an end in himself. This is the great moral advance above Greek and Roman culture, which recognized this moral freedom only in some men. That all men are equal before the law is a high value which is inseparable from a lawful state of right. The moral law establishes this equality of citizens as moral persons. This does not preclude but rather presupposes natural inequalities of physical strength, talents, sex, and age; or of social inequalities of many concrete stations of life and their corresponding duties.

In short: Freedom is not natural but is the result and the consciousness of the profoundest spiritual principle.

In its *negative sense* freedom negates and repels arbitrary and external dominations of the will and unjust, lawless treatment. In its *subjective sense* freedom is the ability to choose one's activities and ends and to participate in common affairs with one's own insight and consent. Formerly, *corporate free-*

doms of particular estates, professions, and cities were legally guaranteed. Such protective laws indeed formulated concrete freedoms and commonly shared, objective values. This is a higher conception than the recent one wherein freedom is only restrictive and laws are so many forms of prohibition. For the latter, freedom is feared and misunderstood as irrational (zufällig) outbursts.

It has also been said that modern states are much too complex to allow freedom as participation in the actions and affairs of all in the state. To which one must reply: Freedom implies variety or inequality, concreteness and complexity of life. And this freedom is made possible through the firmness of law and through the comprehensiveness of the political order in modern states. A well-ordered state also may be trusted to keep this freedom in bounds. But this political condition of freedom is frequently forgotten or taken for granted. Subjective freedom, to be safe in one's property, to have moral responsibility, to cultivate one's talents and good qualities, to gain insight and conviction—presupposes the objective freedom anchored in constitutional laws of the state. Restrictions of freedom become necessary only when freedom is misunderstood and abused by men enmeshed in unmeasurable ambitions or in dissatisfied vanity. Political freedom, on the other hand, is only one aspect within a comprehensive whole which is actual or alive in every member. (Here the famous passage from the preface of Hegel's Philosophy of Law comes to mind: Was vernünftig ist, das ist wirklich; und was wirklich ist, das ist vernünftig. This should be translated: A comprehensive social ethics is actual in every living member, and actual ethical life is possible in comprehensive wholes. The usual translation: "The rational is the real, the real is the rational" is misleading. Re-translated into Hegel's German, it would read: Das Verständige ist das Reale, das Reale ist des Verständige—which indeed is Hegel's definition of rationalism, termed unphilosophical in method as well as in content." (XVII. 112)

§440

The constitution abstractly expresses the concrete enduring form of the state as a comprehensive and organic whole which persists through the changing governments and the natural generations of the people. The state thus should not be confused with an abstract formal law on the one hand and a natural aggregate of many individuals on the other hand. The state, further, is not a voluntary contract between individuals—as if it were a club, whose members may voluntarily join or leave. The individual is born into it without his consent and receives his rights and duties by virtue of it and with his consent.

In spite of its finitude, the state is a self-comprehending ethical substance-subject, and is thus a manifestation of the absolute Concept; it is not possible arbitrarily to will it or not to will it.

§441 (§535)

The ethical objective mind comprehends itself as a universal living state of affairs (Wesen) in which the individual loyalty of all citizens (§431) is just as essential, as its particular formations in professional spheres of activities; its universality includes the independent moral subjects, their welfare and their free will (§435), right of the family, and the legal orders of property. It must secure its political integrity against partisan particularism and cannot tolerate being exploited by private interests.

As ethical substance the state unites in its comprehensiveness the feeling of love nurtured in the family as feeling of patriotism, the common work of business and labor, and administrative functions. Its *highest and absolute end is that personal sub-*

jectivity which knows and wills this concrete uni-versality as its own objective value.

PHILOSOPHY OF HISTORY

§442

The ethical objective mind is actual in many groups of people. In its immediate existence each group is determined by its geographical-climatic conditions and natural resources. Responding to these natural preconditions, the life of a people unfolds in many levels of a maturing process in which the national souls develop, constitute, and comprehend themselves.

§443

Taken in their immediacy, individuals are mutually exclusive of one another; in abstraction from the social matrix, their relationship is external. The whole for them is an abstraction from reality without actuality. The state as an abstract item of reason (Verstandestaat) ought to govern a reality which is external to it. This abstract ought, however, leaves undetermined an equally abstract reality—its content consists of individual whims and irrationalities (Zufall).

§444 (§545)

The state, in and for itself, is an ethical organism. Seen from the outside or externally, however, it appears to others as natural power. This externality or mutual exclusiveness leads to lawless quarrels and to violence: The state of war. The sacrifice of individual lives for the independence of their state establishes the military service as a general institution

(Stand), objectifying the virtue of *courage*. War thus demonstrates that a state is an ethical whole, but one which remains tied to mere natural conditions that divide and exclude peoples from each other.

§445

This naturalistic negativity, which plunges peoples into war, is *self-destructive:* Mere natural existence and immediacy of passion, both unworthy of man, are both called into play and are shaken and destroyed. His immersion in external existence and property, causing wars, in turn makes for the sacrifice of the very naturalistic outlook which brings on war in the first place. In this self-contradictory self-destruction, man makes the experience that he has delivered himself to that which is nil and vain; war is the annihilation of its own nihilism, thus preparing the possibility of peace and the preservation of the ethical whole in a mutual recognition of freedom (Gesinnung der Freiheit).

§446

If the outcome of war results in a mutual recognition of free peoples, *peace is a covenant which ought to be eternal;* but war may also end with the subjugation of one people by another, the first having preferred mere survival to freedom (§355).

§447

Only in the first situation, that of the mutual respect of states for their freedom, is a peace possible, which prevents unilateral actions. External treaties between states which are not critically founded on this principle of good will, remain uncertain *make-*

255

shifts without ethical actuality. Such compromises, further, confuse the actuality of states with individual governments representing them momentarily.

§448

The finite objective mind further is not only conditioned by the externality of nature, but also by *time*. Its temporality is its own history. Peoples have their restricted moments of significance. As thus restricted they enter universal history in which every nation contributes and in which every nation is transcended. In this temporal dialectic of particular national minds, each is appreciated or valued in its contribution to human culture as a whole. This valuation is not subjective opinion but consists in that particular contribution which every people is and does, or fails to be and do. No single people can express the meaning of human history. History comprehensively understood is the judgment on history discreetly understood. (Die Weltgeschichte ist das Weltgericht).

§449 (§549)

History is the development of the finite worldly mind (Weltgeist) in its totality as it unfolds itself and becomes conscious of itself in its temporal development. In this movement the ethical substance of every particular culture is transcended; and the human mind thus realizes its own Concept. Each people occupies one stage or level (Stufe) in the whole movement, and plays in this its own spatial-temporal boundary one scene of the drama.

Philosophy of history must think history as a comprehensive process unfolding itself in finite and concrete teleological wholes (§154)—in religious language, as providence. The discovery of freedom in all its manifestations is the final cause (Endzweck) of history; history is made by freedom and in freedom. At the same time, freedom is historical and becomes conscious of itself as such.

Philosophical comprehension of history as the struggle of finite objective minds to find and express their modifications of freedom, safeguards history *against arbitrary constructions a priori,* which are the inevitable pitfalls of all unphilosophical historians. The latter approach history with one-sided or even fictitious points of view of their own: They assume that history is the fall from an original perfection, or an inevitable progress, and the like. Philosophy, further, saves the dignity of history from the blind empiricism of dry factual details, from psychologistic opinions or guesses, and from pragmatistic shortsighted external teleology. All of these, in view of the whole history, are sheer rubbish (Auskehricht).

Impartiality and objectivity which keep close to the sources are not lukewarm indifference; the historical attitude is rather like the impartiality and objectivity of a judge who makes right his supreme concern, implying a sympathetic understanding of the claims of opposite contributions.

History could not be thought, if the historian could not reconstruct collective actions from objective purposes motivating the agents.

In *political history,* such an objective purpose is the internal and external life of the state—its rise and decline, in distinction from its natural side. A people considered as a mere aggregate and succession of individuals without this unifying ethical whole, which is the state, has no history.

The state in turn makes possible *history of culture* (Bildung), which is the spirit of each historical time. This spirit of culture is expressed in distinct characters and great events; they are intuitively grasped in their significance.

If they see their *individuals* and do not lose themselves in psychological details, then *biographers* and historical novels may gain and express such historical significance against the foils of time and cultures. The center of history is the objective ethical mind struggling for its freedom. But absolute spirit also has its historical side. *History of philosophy*, for example, is concerned with the struggle for truth; *history of religion* and of the church is concerned with the faith in, and the worship of, the Absolute.

History as a whole, then, is the progression in the consciousness of freedom. (Not "progress," which belongs to mechanical techniques. I, p. 41.) This moving spirit of history does not hover above it, but is the painful labor in all those concrete shapes which it moves and changes, gradually becoming aware of its potentiality and its many actualities, transforming its own past achievements into obstacles and stepping stones for its future.

§450

Actualized freedom is the highest and absolute freedom (Recht) of history. When a people becomes aware of a new and decisive possibility of freedom and when it gives it objective expression in action, institution, and arts, for this moment the value (Recht) of other peoples is superseded and becomes an historical past. But no such achievement lasts forever. It disintegrates internally and falls prey to historical contingencies and is sure to be superseded by others. (This § sounds obnoxious, if it is translated literally and taken out of context: "The will of other people has no right (rechtlos) against this absolute will." It must be remembered, however, that "right" is not used in any legal or naturalistic sense, but as manifestation of ethical freedom (cf §415). Hegel thinks of transitions of political power or cultural value from one place or time to another: When Rome took over, Greece had lost its "right." When the

258

Germanic peoples took over, Rome had lost its "right." All this seemingly brutal passage means to say is: "The spirit bloweth where it listeth.")

§451 (§551)

History is actual in and through individual agents. They serve their objective causes with subjective passion (§392). From the point of view of their causes, they are instrumental. They sacrifice their private happiness. Their reward is historical fame and glory—a subjective image generally held or a distorted opinion of how a hero appears to the public (eine formelle Allgemeinheit subjektiver Vorstellung).

§452 (§552)

The whole finite mind lives in the dread of death. To free itself from this anxiety is equivalent to the overcoming the barriers of its singular immediacy. In taking into itself the anxiety of this mortal world, mind transcends it to contemplate the universal and infinite. Concurrently the Absolute becomes the concern of the self-conscious Concept, and the Absolute objectifies or realizes its true infinity in finite or non-absolute agents. Actuality, then, is in its Concept, and the Concept is absolutely actual.

TRANSITION FROM OBJECTIVE MIND TO ABSOLUTE SPIRIT

Objective mind as it exists concretely in politically unified nations is a non-ending dialectical struggle which never reaches absolute finality. It is a struggle with natural necessities and with external conditions. One-sided and restricted in every people, it is subject to irrationality (Zufall) and to subconscious habits or modes of behavior. It is also a struggle for temporal survival against catastrophic nature and against the hostile world. All this limits the historical world-spirit as actualized in many exclusive peoples, cultures, and states. In looking back and contemplating the achievements of history and their sad limitations, mind rises in this contemplation above them and elevates itself to the truth of the absolute spirit, which is not bound by subjective and historical minds. Stripped of its worldliness objective mind becomes a knowing comprehension, free in and for itself as united with the Absolute—in the light of which nature and history, necessity and purpose, serve its revelation and are vessels of its glory.

The logical forms involved in this elevation of the world as mind to God, in mutual inter-activity was dealt with in the systematic introduction to the *Logic* (§25). The elevation of the finite to the infinite was at the same time shown to be an actualization of the infinite in its non-absolute finitude.

The logical nerve (Moment) of this double mediation is the dialectical *negation:* As soon as nature and history are known in their finitude, they are transcended. Being as a whole transcends them, but in transcending them remains immanent in them. Both may be immediate starting points of a purifying and introscending movement, in which they are restored and justified as being mediated in and by this movement.

This movement of the mind is a self-purgation; the mind cleanses itself from mere opinions and scientific theories, and from selfish desires and political practices. This struggle is actual in history: History both *is* and *overcomes* its own inadequacies.

From the concrete actuality of the finite ethical sphere (Sittlichkeit) emerges the idea of God or the Absolute. The free spirit finds its absoluteness in religion, which includes ethics as its necessary precondition. It is vain to look for a true religion outside and apart from ethics.

Although ethics is autonomous in itself—independent of religion—it nevertheless reaches its absolute ground and justification only in religion. While in practice it may seem to exclude religion, it nevertheless is included in religion. The priority of religion is mediated through ethics—when ethics begins to realize its incompetence and confesses its finitude, its religious ground is reached.

Kant is quite right when he says that the cosmological proof of the existence of God: Proving him *ex contingentia mundi,* or from the non-absoluteness of the given world; and the physico-teleological proof: Proving him from the non-absoluteness of finite purposes—are negative proofs: They require a positive content which can be found in the free and comprehensive spirit of the ethical sphere, Kant's *practical reason.*

The Concept of freedom is identical with an all-comprehensive self-determining Absolute, which negates any finite fixation as final (§40).

Kant, however, degrades his true insight, when he reduces the Absolute to a mere *postulate* or *ought* of practical reason. The ought characterizes, as was shown (§172), the situation of infinite moral subjects. To apply this category of morality to the Absolute is misdirected. It is, on the contrary, the insight into the incompetence of morality—the finite moral person is never as he ought to be—which leads to the realization of the Absolute in which the finite incompetence is posited, cancelled, and preserved in the eternal life of God.

In history, the dialectical tension between the objective and the absolute spirit appears in the dialectical relation of *state* and *church:* It is an enormous mistake either to separate these inseparable opposites or to identify them or to declare that they are indifferent to one another. Their abstract separation deprives the state of the absolute justification of its ethical core; instead of comprehending the state in its ethical actuality, disfigured by natural contingencies and psychical irrationalities, and as limited by other states in space and time, the state is said to be nothing but secular based on might and violence alone. Religion then is tolerated as a mere subjective, private affair, apart from political right.

On the other hand, religion, particularly in the Roman Catholic church, perverts the absolute spirit into an external organization or into magic objects. In the "Host" God is presented to the worshipper as identical with an external object. All other external, unfree, non-spiritual superstitions are implied in this primary and supreme mistake of externalization. The *layman* is made dependent on the *clergy* from which he is to procure his *knowledge* of the absolute, and by which his conscience is to be guided; the clergy, in turn, receive their consecration not spiritually but by an external tradition and a magical act. Others are begged and bribed to pray for people or to represent them before God. Miracle-working images, holy bones, and external works of others whose merits may even be transferred to their account, etc. —all this perverts the absolute spirit and fetters it in naturalistic categories of a being which is external to itself; whereby right and justice, social ethics and moral conscience, responsibility and duty are ruined in their very roots. Lack of freedom, political laws and constitutions correspond to this consistent denial of all freedom in religion. The Roman Catholic church has been praised for securing stability of governments—indeed! But such governments as are connected with despotism, corruption, and barbarism; they do not recognize that to be free and dedicated to the right is the ethical principle of all citizens.

Lurking beneath such an ecclesiastic totalitarianism is an abstract secular political fanaticism which is only prevented from bursting into the open by lawless suppression and immoral coercion. Catholic states thus are constantly tossed from one abstract undialectical extreme to another.

The same incompatibility is present in the *Roman Catholic ethics:* Ethical values are alienated and taken out of self-consciousness. They are replaced by an institutionalized saintliness which negates the actual life in the state. The ethical dignity of *marriage* is devalued by the "higher" institutionalized *chastity* of priests, monks, and nuns; the diligence, work and activity, by which *property* is acquired, is abrogated by the "higher" institutionalized vow of *poverty;* this is a contradiction in itself for in that one give away his property to the other he enriches the other. Instead of *honesty* in transactions and intelligent participation in common concerns of the community, a *blind obedience* to authorities without right or duty is demanded. In summary: The enslavement of conscience inevitably follows, if saintliness is put above ethics. It is foolish and vain to expect a political ethics to be valid and respected, if it is subordinated to a religion to which there is no sanctity in ethics. Under such conditions, conscience cannot be bound by political constitutions or institutions when their religious justification is absent. A mere secular revolution cannot be the basis of a political freedom if there is no concomitant reformation of religion. It is only an unreliable makeshift to declare the rights of men, and the independence of secular rights and laws from religion, when this freedom of mind is incapable of pervading to pervade and appropriating the depth of the religious spirit and elevating itself to its truth. Even if the laws are truly ethical, they must always be in jeopardy as long as the religious background is incompatible with them. Another lame compromise is the saying: Give to the emperor what is the emperor's and to God what is God's. The question is precisely to think the unity of these opposites and the right of their respective spheres within this unity. (Hegel's criticism is too much rooted in the Renaissance and Reformation, for whom the "dark ages" were something to be skipped. Hegel underrates Thomas Aquinas, for example.)

The absolute validity of right and justice, duty and moral law, are well founded only if they participate in the truth of the absolute spirit; the state in turn is but the external appearance of this freedom. The whole concrete sphere of ethics is one manifestation of the divine spirit in the self-conscious actuality of a people and of each individual thereof. Religion and ethics, although distinct, are nevertheless inseparable. There are not two different consciences, a moral one and a religious one. As moral, conscience faces outward actualities; on its religious side, it knows itself as anchored in the Absolute, which sanctifies moral activity in the world. Religious freedom and moral political freedom guarantee each other.

If the objective mind and the absolute spirit are not distinguished as well as united, the result is either a pseudo-absolutization of the state—political fanaticism; or a pseudo-political church as a coercive institution—ecclesiastic totalitarianism.

Plato was the first philosopher who saw the profound conflict of inner freedom and eternal justice with existing political conditions; and the conflict of the moral law with the polytheism of poetic imagination. The task of philosophy as he saw it, was to discover those truly universal principles of justice which are the ground of true constitutions and of political life; without which there is no diminishing the evils which beset states and plague mankind. Plato's Idea is the free thought which determines itself for itself and is universally valid for all consciences. His state as an ethical whole ("substance") however, was not seen yet as existing in the individual subject in whom and for whom the Idea is actual. He fails to see that the actualization of the Idea in the individual is just as essential as the Idea itself. This is the advance made beyond Plato's justice in Aristotle's Entelechy as the substantial core of the state. The state is for itself in the individual and it is for the individual in itself. While the individual is not the whole, and the whole is not the individual, the one is nevertheless not without the other. Together they are one dialectical identity, mediated by their difference.

Plato's state does not yet contain this, its own opposite; the infinite subjective freedom was still hidden from his vision. He did not grasp the dialectical identity of every subject with the eternal substance (§416). His state, therefore, remained in the form of thought, in contrast to the corruption of all empirical states—as summarized in the famous passage: As long as philosophers do not reign in the states, or as long as those who are called kings and rulers do not have a profound and all-embracing (umfassend) philosophy, so long will there be no emancipation from evils for states or for human-kind. Philosophy is not only for the rulers, but for every man.

The Idea as absolute spirit appeared in the absolute religion of Christianity. Here freedom, which is both absolute and empirical, is grasped as the essential ethical actuality of every human subject. However, this absolute religion could not have appeared had not philosophy prepared its ground and purified thought as identical with the absolute being, which is both in itself as well as for itself.

The actuality of the spirit incessantly strives to overcome itself in order to realize its dialectical nature; its absolute freedom is one in religious conscience and in philosophical self-knowledge. Philosophy thus—as Plato failed to realize—knows itself to be one of the limited forms of the absolute spirit; it is only one form of absolute truth. (It seems to me that Hegel speaks here not so much about Plato, but rather defends himself against the accusation that all other forms of life are swallowed by philosophy.)

Absolute religion concurrently also has its immediate or irrational aspect. It also must develop distinctions in its Idea. In its immediate and one-sided appearance it has been falsely identified with the existence of this sensuously and externally given individual (Jesus) thus resulting in the suppression of the freedom of the spirit and the perversion of political life. But its principle contains the infinite and absolute form of subjectivity in agreement with its eternal substance. This principle is bound to repel its perversions and to develop its implication: To become that free spirit which knows its comprehensiveness and truth, actualizing the unity of religious and ethical conscience—the principle of *Protestantism.*

The original principle of absolute religious means that it must go beyond its immediacy (§41). The religious and ethical spirit must actualize itself in everyday activities as well as in the constitutions and life of the state. The religious spirit and the ethical meaning of the state are the only firm guarantees of a good life, when they mutually respect each other and co-operate." (X. 433-445)

ABSOLUTE SPIRIT

§453

The soul in its immediacy is irrational (begriffos). This is a necessary side of objective mind; in turn objective mind gains its absolute justification in the absolute spirit, not in itself. All finite movements of the spirit are stations on its way; absolute spirit lingers in each while pressing on to gain its real existence and freedom by leaving them behind. A chain of exploded systems marks the fiery path of the absolute spirit. The Concept of the absolute Idea in *Logic* is the ontological category, being actualized and achieving existence in existence in absolute spirit. In actuality, absolute spirit appears in the forms (Gestalten) of art, religion, and philosophy, all of which at their best are worthy of the Concept. In each of them, free and actual intelligence grasps its identity with the dialectical essence of the world; it exists not only as achievement of a past, but also as the presence of the eternal Now in an educational process of self-liberation and self-articulation (herausbildet).

§454 (§554)

The dialectical negation of single individuals in their living immediacy mediates their participation in the life of an objective whole; this necessary participation is identical with a free dedication. The ethical community rests on such sacrificial life of all its members. This life of sacrifice, is, further, the ethical root of philosophy. All worldly existence is posited by and in the Absolute; it is also sacrificed for the sake of the Absolute in its eternal life. Philosophical contemplation, in thinking this through, participates in the sacrificial life of the Absolute; like the Absolute, it transcends the dialectical essence of nature as well as of finite mind.

Absolute spirit is the living and actual identity of the eternal being which *is what it is in itself,* but which also is its own eternal self-differentiation, eternally re-absorbed by itself. As this absolute knowledge, absolute spirit is this process *for itself.*

Religion represents this same process and this absolute knowledge in the medium of faith; on the one hand, faith begins in the feeling of the finite subject and is not found outside of it; on the other hand, God absolutely establishes himself in the community of faith as their absolute ground; the absolute spirit is evident to the spirit of the faithful.

In recent times this interplay of absoluteness and its corresponding subjective response has been minimized: One only refers to religion as subjective state of mind or as a piety immanent in feeling and as anthropological projection. In contrast to this subjectivism as well as to objectivistic dogmatism, philosophy comprehends a truly religious faith as a form of absolute truth (§455, §553-§555).

ART

(Hegel changed the title of the first edition: *The Religion of Art* to *Art,* second edition.)

§456 (§556)

The aesthetic *Ideal,* called Beauty, is the absolute spirit immediately presented to the senses and to imagination. All arts imitate the Ideal.

Natural materials are rendered unessential in the art of the Ideal; they are transparent expressions of the absolute idea. The artistic spirit works out (einbildend) its imagination in symbolic media. In this transfiguration of the material into a symbol all foreignness is overcome. The shape of beauty in a work of art shows nothing but its own perfection. It does not point beyond itself (as scientific and practical languages always do).

The finite aspect of art remains tied to its natural media or carriers. Thus, separate works of art are scattered in space and time. This external existence of art brings about a distance between the work—in itself a shaped living whole (Gestalt) born from and expressive of spirit—and the creative artists, and congenial admirers and appreciators.

(The term "Ideal," in distinction from "Idea," is derived from Kant. He defines the Ideal as an absolute concrete whole which is unique and completely self-determined, an absolute individuality. On the subjective side, Kant determines the Ideal as the free interplay of all faculties of the soul; or as a symbolic fusion of soul and body, subject and object, in a work which leaves nothing to be desired and which is enjoyed with "disinterested interest."

Hegel takes it for granted that his reader knows Kant's aesthetics. He goes beyond Kant in that the aesthetic Idea is ontologically real and true: It is the sensuous mirror of a speculative truth. The totality of dialectic opposites is symbolically presented. It is both a symbol of life and a symbol of perfection and totality. The interplay of all functions of life is at the same time, in its form, a symbol of finality, absoluteness, totality.)

§457 (§557)

Beauty is the immediate unity of nature and spirit in the form of intuition (Anschauung). In Greek culture it appears in the gods, which are universal powers pervading both the world of nature and the world of man, shaped and presented in and for imagination. The aesthetic gods are naturalized spirits and spirited natures in immediate and individual balances; they determine and are the content of the arts. On the one hand, they overcome the negativity of the finite and natural phenomena. On the other hand, they elevate and absorb the subject in their divine life. Although these gods are blessed in themselves, they nevertheless lack the revelation of the absolute in the subject as such. The aesthetic community gathered in their honor, therefore lacks the depth of conscience. It is nevertheless a spiritual community by virtue of the absolute ideality of art. Freedom is enjoyed as the freedom to play with all contents of life. Beauty unites men without moral obligation or coercion.

§458 (§558)

No art imitates nature. It fuses external, given, natural materials as well as internal, given, subjective imagination and self-expressions. It may speak the language of nature, making use of natural materials, shapes, and movements, but only insofar as they lend themselves to express spiritual contents which art feels forshadowed (ahnen) in them. The human shape is the highest natural form because the spirit shines through the living body of man and expresses itself immediately through expressive gestures. It is in analogy to this that art takes other natural shapes, sights, and scenes as significant, characteristic, and meaningful perceptions.

We say that the elementary and concrete life of nature as well as all value concerns of human culture are collected in the aesthetic gods. Pure thinking of philosophy, however, cannot remain satisfied with this aesthetic polytheism of imagination. It is driven beyond the aesthetic sphere and must realize its value as well as its limitation. The absolute spirit cannot fully explicate itself in the indefinite plurality of shapes.

§459 (§559)

Works of art, further, are limited by different styles of different peoples and periods, yet art remains art in every style. Its intuitive inner-penetration of image and spirit may transfigure any given content at any given time. By virtue of this, its aesthetic form, even the most unessential and fleeting contents or occasions may enter works of art. Art is the great liberation from natural immediacies, and lifts life above itself in the very language of life. The beautiful expression in all styles is blessed in itself (durch ihn selbst verklärt); it is indifferent to its external occasions.

§460 (§560)

The perfect fusion of thought and image in beauty is a concrete form of the absolute spirit. It creates archetypes (vorbildicher Gedanke) in spite of its infinitely diverse contents.

Through the aesthetic *genius* archetypes are inspired by and correspond to the aesthetic arts. The seizure by the god is known as enthusiasm; overcoming the artist as if it were an alien power. This immediate creativeness is something he suffers (Pathos). What he produces, the work of art, is a gift of the god, when no subjective whims and reflections are mixed in. Creative activity is one with the objective value (Gehalt) which it creates.

The genius is different from the *artist* in him who makes something according to technical rules and who has to accommodate himself according to the requirements of communication; this requires diligence, work, and technical understanding. The genius is not free to choose or reject his vision; but the artist is free to choose his way of handling the vision.

The work thus is inspired by the god and is the product of conscious deliberate choice.

Classical beauty rests serene and blessed in its perfect equilibrium and reconciliation of appearing image and spiritual expression, unaware of the negativity in the absolute in which no sensuous appearance is final and real in and for itself. *Sublime* beauty reveals this discrepancy. The immeasurably great is felt in the inadequacy of the sensuous medium to express it fully.

Archaic (symbolische) beauty is still striving to find an adequate expression for a vaguely felt content. It creates monstrous allegorical shapes, tossing restlessly from the extreme of abstract formalism to the other extreme of unmediated sensuality. (Hegel took the term "symbolic" for archaic art from a work of his friend, Friedrich Creuzer: *Symbolik und Mythologie der alten Völker*. I think this is an unfortunate choice of a term because it is central to all things aesthetic; all art is symbolic.)

§462 (§562)

The artist in sacrificing himself unconditionally to the production of his work is purified. His subjective pecularities are extinguished and atoned for in the birth-pang of his objective presentation in which his true self is present. If he is a genius he expresses the truest spirit of his people. The aesthetic gods of his people speak through his mouth.

The painful practice and labor of the artist is preserved but also forgotten in the finished presence of his substantial opus; the mediating work returns to a new and higher immediacy.

When his people participate in the lofty revelation of a divine vision, expressed in the art of the genius, they share with him the same meaning of aesthetic liberation; a freedom from and above mere life. The accomplished freedom of the spirit is objectified, beheld, and enjoyed. The aesthetic way of life is, therefore, a way of salvation from the unfree finitudes of natural life and practical existence. Art is thus doing in its own medium of sensuous imagination what philosophy does in thought. The presentation of the interplay of all opposites is common to both. In other words, the aesthetic liberation is only one level or kind of freedom, not freedom in and for itself. The highest form of freedom knows itself as such; *it is one with the absolute respect* (Ehrfurcht) *for the depth of the person.*

Greek art was indistinguishable from an art-religion. Art as a religion had a metaphysical significance which it lost in the Christian period. Its *romantic* art (Hegel thinks of Dante or the Gothic cathedral) cannot present God adequately in sensuous form. Religious inwardness remains beyond its appearance which merely alludes to it. This leads to an allegorical art, as in mystery plays, in which sensuous appearance has no necessary unity with that to which it merely points.

Pictures, thus worshipped, may therefore be ugly idols; even holy bones may serve this abstract allegorical purpose better than beautiful pictures and are more likely to work miracles.

§464 (§563)

In history, Art-religion was superseded by the absolute religion, which was its future. Here spirit reveals itself as absolute spirit to spirit and is no longer confined to the many aesthetic gods of imagination and to their mythical tales.

(Much has been said against Hegel's alleged contention that art has no future. A careful reading of his section and corresponding passage in his philosophy of art shows, of course, that he has said nothing of the sort. All he means to say is that art is no longer art-religion, that art is no longer the exclusive or final organ for the Absolute. The interpretation that Hegel had "stopped art" belongs to the Hegel legend.)

RELIGION

(Hegel's philosophy of religion hinges on the term *Vorstellung*. It means, first, an introduction of one person to another; second, a performance of a play or, third, a symbolic representation of a value, as a scepter and crown represents the value of royal dignity; fourth, a general concept of empirical things which could be illustrated in pictures; fifth, something that stands over against me. In order to distinguish the religious *Vorstellung* from other types, Hegel calls it mythical; and in the myth he distinguishes two basic types: The poetic myth as found in Homer, and the quasi-historical myth as it is found in the Biblical tradition. We are now in the position to understand his central definition of religion: Religion is the Absolute in the form of mythical tale and performance (Religion ist das Absolute in der Form der Vorstellung). The mythical language of religion personifies the Absolute so that the spiritual relation as between persons becomes possible in prayer and cult. This distinguishes the religious form of the absolute spirit from the two impersonal forms in art and in philosophy.

I follow the development of Hegel's religious philosophy from its first simple formulations in the *Propädeutik*, before I take up the few condensed sections in the Encyclopedia.)

INTRODUCTION FROM THE PROPADEUTIK

§71-80 and §207

The moral law in us is the eternal law of Reason (Vernunft) which we are bound to respect, and by which we are bound indissolubly. This Absolute moral ought immediately reveals the inadequacy of our individuality in the light of it. In this, our incompetence, we acknowledge moral Reason as something higher than we are, as an independent and autonomous essential being (Wesen). It reveals itself in our pure consciousness of it; it communicates itself in and through our knowledge of it. This double mediation—through our incompetence and through the competent knowledge of our incompetence—when grasped or felt in its immediacy may be called *faith*.

Knowledge of the Absolute cannot but be absolute knowledge of itself. To put it negatively: It can have nothing finite as its positing or justifying ground, nor can it be proved through something outside of it, which is not absolute.

The negative mediation of absolute knowledge is, seen from our finitude, an elevation above it; we must start from our sensuous and finite nature in order to transcend it and recognize it in its mortality and metaphysical worthlessness (Nichtigkeit).

Since absolute knowledge is this movement, it must not remain in its immediacy as an inner feeling or as a vague faith in an indefinite abstract being-in-general, but must proceed to comprehend the Absolute in the mythical term "God." To know God is not above comprehension, but *is* above reason which is the knowledge of things finite and relative. Comprehension is the responsive reflection (Widerschein) on God and of God.

Religion brings God close to a people's minds in mythical representations, involving feelings and thoughts. In worship the religious mind forgets itself and also forgets the mediating means of its elevation; it is unaware of the particular imagery which is necessarily connected with cultic actions honoring the absolute relation of man to God. *God is the absolute spirit:* In its non-mythical truth, it is the pure dialectical essence of all Being which objectifies itself in its own otherness, by means of which it returns eternally to itself; it maintains its identity in and through its non-absolute and finite self-manifestations.

God is *holy* is that absolute whole which has nothing alien outside of itself; which has no "temptation." He is absolute *power* insofar as he actualizes its concrete wholeness in all individuations: In mythical language, He is the "creator" of his "creation." The Absolute is *wisdom* as its power is one with its holiness. The Absolute is *good* as it bestows freedom to the individuals; and *just* as it eternally reunites all individuals in its eternal life.

Sin (das Böse) is alienation from God. The human individual abuses his freedom in declaring his independence from the whole and in striving and clinging to his finite exclusiveness as if he were absolute in and for himself.

But this very freedom to sin, is and remains nevertheless a divine gift. Even in evil, the divine and human nature are not totally alienated. This truth assures man of divine *grace*. He may grasp it whereby the reconciliation of God with the world comes to pass and the alienation of man from God is cancelled.

To "serve God" means that the individual strives to effect this unity with God, not only by concentrating his thoughts and feelings on him in order to receive the assurance of being affirmed in the divine will, but also by proving in its actual life with other individuals that his will and intention is in conformity with the divine will.

Religion "introduces" (vorstellen) the absolute spirit not only in terms of imagination and mythical representation, and as ground for personal-moral value, but also for thought and true knowledge. Logical contemplation also lifts the individual to the thought of the Absolute, and ascertains his unity with it.

Religion makes this truth available to all men in various degrees of comprehension. Its essence is religious love, the law and dynamics of religious existence. Love is actual in readiness for others: In this meeting of persons, human wills are acknowledged and honored in their truth (§358 Enc.). Religious love is thus not only an affection for things, or moral benevolence or a vague feeling; it proves itself in absolute sacrifice: "Love each other as I have loved you." It is the infinite power of all that is finite and thus triumphs over bad, evil, crime, and positive law. Divine love forgives sin. It undoes past doings: Mary Magdalene is forgiven because she has loved. Religious love is beyond morality: Maria annoints Christ, instead of using the money for the poor, and Christ approves. Forgiveness of sin is the core of man's relationship to God: I identify myself with this divine love and accept myself in this knowledge that God is love. Love is not something temporal—as restoration of honor follows an external punishment—but an eternal truth in and for the spirit. The love of God for man and the love of man for God *is* the eternal life in which one's temporal nothingness is both annihilated and affirmed. It is an illusion of unenlightened, representational, object-thinking to project this eternal life into a "beyond," separated from our life here.

In the Christian religion this identity of divine and human life is beheld in the Christ myth: "The son of man is the son of God;" for him there is no beyond: "I and the father are one." He is thus the true religious man. The external story of this historical life must be distinguished from its religious significance. Christ has experienced the ignominious meanness of life, has taken it upon himself and sacrificed himself for it. His sorrow in life affirms, in religious suffering, the unity of divine and human nature.

The blessed Gods of the Greeks were pictured as

dwelling beyond this life: Through Christ God sanctifies this life. The myth of his resurrection and ascension to "the right hand of God," as Stephanus envisaged it, is evident to faith: It means God's eternal life being one with temporal life and eternally returning to itself. It is trifling and pitiful to deny or doubt its religious meaning from the point of view of historical circumstances and details as if it were an external fact. Faith is not concerned with sensuous facts but with God's history, which happens eternally.

This eternal division and reconciliation of God and man is known and "performed" (vorgestellt) in the *church*: This is the holy spirit of the community reflected in the holy image. The holy spirit is not a contingent, arbitrary decree of external authority. The invisible church of the holy spirit embraces all continents and different religions. Only secondarily is it an institutional church with specific symbols. In the Roman Catholic church, especially, the community of faith is split in priests and laymen. The former have authority and rule by coercion. The reconciliation of God is rendered external, depriving religion of spiritual actuality. For the Protestants, priests are only teachers. All members of the community are equal before God, whose spirit is present in the community of faith. Without faith and good will (Gesinuung) works as such are without merit. The actual community with God can take place only in the depths of the soul, transfiguring the sensuous forms of sacraments.

§465 (§564)

The whole reveals its essential dialectical structure in nature and in spirit as partial manifestations of itself. As absolute spirit, the whole is this dialectic for itself. Religion as a special form of the absolute spirit pictures and dramatizes the ontological dialectic of the Absolute in a sequence of mythical tales and performances.

In the mythical language of religion, truth is revealed by God to the divine spirit in man. God discloses himself in the personal self-consciousness of man, of which he is the absolute ground. Conversely, man's religious knowledge is not only a personal knowledge about God; it is also man's knowing himself in God.

Reason's contention, that God is unknowable, flatly contradicts the first principle of religion; God has revealed himself. This modern agnosticism corresponds to a primitive conception of religion, against which Plato and Aristotle have protested that God is not envious. To understand the proposition: "God is absolute spirit," the whole of speculative philosophy is required. Faith is satisfied with its symbolic images and performances. Abstract reason can but dissect these and point out the obvious inconsistencies in them. True thought will nevertheles proceed to comprehend them.

§466 (§566)

The Absolute is the One which distinguishes its many contrary spheres within itself; manifests itself in that which it is not and which eternally restores its fulness and unity in and through and out of its appearing and individuated processes.

Religion is one of the many contrary spheres. Religion is a particular form of the absolute spirit, with a language of its own, in which the Absolute is pictured, worshipped, personified, and performed.

§467

The Absolute as universal world ground, as substantial power, justice and wisdom in the universe is presented in religious language as remaining One in its otherness, and represented as "the Son." And as eternally resurrecting and restoring its eternal life through the death of all things finite and individuated, the Absolute is mythically known as the "holy ghost."

§468

Reason is blind to the Absolute: Its world falls apart in elementary life and organic nature, the skies and the earth; its finite mind falls apart in abstract forms, external to content; and it stands in external opposition to an object over against it. If reason clings to this existential negativity of the finite as if it were absolute, it absolutizes its own nothingness for which it claims independence. To claim independence, however, for something which is absolutely dependent, is a metaphysical lie; or ethically speaking, this is the radical evil of the finite mind. (Hegel might have added that in mythical language this is referred to as the "devil.")

§469 (§569)

The Absolute is not only the essential ground of world-spheres such as nature and history; it is also the ground of each individual in his personal uniqueness. In Christian language: The "only begotten son" lives in a certain historical time.

The metaphysical lie and radical evil is this: A finite will pretends to play God. This existential untruth does not touch or remove the ontological truth that the mortal individual is dependent upon, cancelled by, and preserved and justified in the eternal Being. Sin, which is negativity and destroys itself, is as nothing in the Absolute; also the Absolute affirms itself in it. It is "the forgiveness of sin." In *repentance*, the infinite sorrow about the negativity of the self is the return to the unbroken wholeness and holiness of the Absolute; in true repentance, the concrete unity of the universal and the individual exist for itself. In mythical Christian language: The "son takes the sin of the world upon himself;" the sin is undone in his absolute sacrifice.

§470

The Christian religion, in its immediacy, falls apart in an empirical-historical Jesus and an equally empirical or "positive" church, which beholds Jesus from the outside as if he were on display. But the religious truth present in the mythical Christ cancels this empirical immediacy: It is sacrificed, overcome, and is known as nothing and evil in itself, if proclaimed as final and authoritative.

If a personal life in and for the eternal truth is taken to be a model for Christian believers, then the believer too will alienate himself from his alienation, i.e. from his natural immediacy, and he too will unite himself with the divine life in the sorrow of negativity, the "cross we have to bear."

In comprehension faith is thus united with the dialectical essence of the Absolute. The absolute spirit is the universal process of mediation actualized and present in the community of faith, the universal, invisible church.

§471

Philosophy thus understands religion as one of its own presuppositions and as a particular articulation of the absolute totality. It sees through the form of mythical representations by virtue of which the life of the Absolute is pictured in seemingly discreet stories, quasi-temporal myths, and cultic symbols.

Philosophy uses such language without being taken captive by it. The revelation of the Absolute is not confined to religion, but can and must also be thought in the logical form of truth. This comprehensive truth corresponds to the comprehensive and eternal actuality of the Absolute in *all* its opposite manifestations.

"In philosophy thought becomes absolutely *free* in and for itself, as it unites itself with the absolute content which is *necessary* in and for itself." (X. 458).

PHILOSOPHY

§472

Philosophy may be said to be the unity of art and religion: Like art, philosophy beholds the unity of opposites in the life of the world; like religion, it transcends all worldly contents in the absolute unity of truth formulated in its own dialectical logic. Unlike art, philosophical intuition cannot be fulfilled in sensuous appearances and particular works; unlike religion, its absolute truth cannot rest in a cycle of mythical representations. Philosophy is the unity of immanent content and transcendent form in free and self-conscious reflection. It justifies the essential difference of its spheres as necessary and its comprehension also comprehends the irrational or the immediate.

§473 (§573)

Philosophy is the liberation of the spirit from the insufficiency and one-sidedness of all forms of life; in passing beyond them, they are nevertheless preserved and ultimately grounded. The whole is a whole of movements maintaining its concrete identity in all its passages. All immediate beginnings are at the same time mediated results.

The whole course of philosophy is based on its own dialectical logic, whose categories unfold all ontological distinctions which pervade the life of nature and of mind. Philosophy moves from immediate or irrational experience, through rational and objectifying experience, to the realm of the absolute spirit in art and in religion, wherein philosophy sees the counterpart of its own Concept in intuitive and mythical symbols. This whole way of liberation is not only a preparation for, or a way toward, philosophy; but is also within philosophy. What it works out, its own Concept, is nothing apart from the process of its continuous self-relation. Ground and end, absolute finality and absolute movement, are the same.

The three forms of the absolute spirit—art, religion, philosophy—represent the same Absolute. They differ only in the medium of expression. All three are ways of salvation from the oppressive and restricting problems of external nature and finite mind.

(In a long footnote to the second edition, Hegel defends his dialectical position against various undialectical positions which are at odds amongst themselves: His position is not *pantheism*, which identifies God and world; it is not *atheism* or *moralism*, which falsely absolutizes finite experiences or moral issues; it is not *theism*, which personifies the Absolute, instead of thinking it as ground of the absolute value of the person; it is not *dualism*, where God and world are absolutely split, as if "creator" would make any sense without "creation;" it is not *akosmism*, where God is all and the world only an illusion (Maya). On the subjective side, it is neither *traditionalism* enslaved to external "revelations" and authorities; nor is it *liberalism* which is blind for absolute religious values in objectified and mythical traditions.)

§474

The *Concept* of philosophy is truth knowing itself, the idea thinking itself, the spirit living its thought. Dialectic, the logic of philosophy, is the explication (Ur-Teil) of the Concept in all essential shapes of life, in nature, soul, mind, and spirit. The movement of these living contents and the movement of dialectical thought is one and the same movement. In space and time it shines through disappearing appearances, founding, transcending, and preserving them in their true meaning.

§475

The Concept and its self-division (Ur-Teil) terminates in three essential "conclusions" in which the three basic metaphysical spheres—the Absolute, nature, mind mediate each other.

Nature as a whole may be the mediating link or metaphysical "middle term," presupposing ontology and making spirit possible.

Spirit, in working out the logic of its objects, makes or produces itself, and discovers its ground in the Absolute (§139).

The idea of the absolute as the "middle" prevents reason from cutting the whole into separate entities. Nature and spirit are aspects of the whole in their mutual interpenetration. (See pictorial diagram in Appendix.)

§476

The second mediation is that of the spirit and implies the standpoint of the knowing subject. By working at nature, it unites itself with ontology.

§477 (§577)

The movements from the whole through nature to spirit, and from nature through spirit to the idea of the whole, are comprehended in comprehension. Philosophy as this total comprehension takes the

286

absolute totality as its center, of which nature and spirit are double aspects. In this concrete totality spirit has a priority over nature, because in spirit totality exists in the form of being known in and for itself whereas nature is the same totality but not aware of itself as such.

The Idea manifests itself in this three-fold self-differentiation, which is both founded in the nature of things and is also the activity of philosophical knowledge. Absolute spirit acts, creates, and enjoys itself in the eternal Idea, which is both in itself and for itself. Comprehension knows itself in Being and Being knows itself in comprehension. (Hegel concluded §577 of the second edition with a quotation in Greek from Aristotle's Metaphysics X.7.)

"And thinking in itself deals with that which is best in itself, and that which is thinking in the fullest sense with that which is best in the fullest sense. And thought thinks on itself because it shares the nature of the object of thought; for it becomes an object of thought in coming into contact with and thinking its objects, so that thought and object of thought are the same. For that which is *capable* of receiving the object of thought, i.e. the essence, is thought. But it is *active* when it *possesses* this object. Therefore the possession rather than the receptivity is the divine element which thought seems to contain, and the act of contemplation is what is most pleasant and best. If the God is always in that good state in which we sometimes are, this compels our wonder; and if in a better this compels it yet more. And God *is* in a better state. And life also belongs to God; for the actuality of thought is life, and God is that actuality; and God's self-dependent actuality is life most good and eternal. We say therefore that God is a living being, eternal, most good, so that life and duration continuous and eternal belong to God; for this *is* God."